sam
the cooking guy

just a bunch of recipes

samzien

WILEY

John Wiley & Sons, Inc.

Published by John Wiley & Sons, Inc., Hoboken, New Jersey
Published simultaneously in Canada

For general information on our other products and services or for technical support, please
contact our Customer Care Department within the United States at (800) 762-2974, outside the
United States at (317) 572-3993 or fax (317) 572-4002.

Wiley also publishes its books in a variety of electronic formats. Some content that appears in
print may not be available in electronic books. For more information about Wiley products, visit
our Web site at www.wiley.com.

Interior design by Howard Klein
Composition by Jeff Baker

Library of Congress Cataloging-in-Publication Data

Zien, Sam.
  Sam the cooking guy: just a bunch of recipes / Sam Zien.
      p. cm.
  Includes index.
  ISBN 978-0-470-04373-8 (pbk.)
  1. Quick and easy cookery. I. Title.
  TX833.5.Z54 2008
  641.5'55—dc22
                            2007013697

Printed in the United States of America

10 9 8 7 6 5 4 3 2

To Kelly

Contents

I've thought about this page a lot and couldn't wait to write it. That's because without the people on this page, there would be no book—literally. You'd just be standing there holding nothing in your hands, *and that would look really silly.*

Justin—for your September 2, 2004, e-mail, which started this. And even though you called my introduction to the proposed chapter on lunch "odd," I want to thank you for what you did.

Mr. and Mrs. Lasher—Mrs. Lasher, I'd say you "made me what I am today," but my mother would have an absolute coronary. So let's go with "you're pretty darn amazing." And to Mr. Lasher, for all the hand-holding and advice on the eleventh commandment. Plus for inspiring me with your words "a cookbook is just a bunch of recipes." You're a genius.

Max, Jordan, and Zach—people are always thanking their kids. But in terms of this book, not only didn't you guys help, but you actually kept me from working on it at times. I love you all dearly, but a thank-you? Boys, you've got to be kidding.

My mom and dad—I didn't realize it at the time, but I probably get my love of cooking from you, Mom—you're the most naturally talented cook I know. And Dad, though you pretty much can't boil water, you did teach me to clean the hell out of my garage. The fact that I choose not to doesn't really matter. I know how, and if I wanted to, I could.

Alberto Pando—the first person who saw something in Sam the Cooking Guy. You laughed, but in a good way. I remember the day you called.

Peg, Sarah, Fontaine—you guys have made so much of this way, way better for me. Thank you.

Karla—for being a fan first, and now my assistant. You rock.

The editor wishes to thank Amy Laskin—without Amy's suggestion to check out Sam the Cooking Guy, I never would have e-mailed Sam that fateful day, and this cookbook might have been published by someone else. *Thanks.*

Introduction

"I can't cook." I hear that all the time. And it's not that you can't—it's that you don't. It's that we've been wrecked by cooking shows with their millions of complicated steps and crazy-ass ingredients. Ingredients you can't find, let alone pronounce. That's not how I want to cook. I want to eat well, but I don't want it to take a year. Who's making stuff like "Truffled Peruvian Mountain Squab with Chilled Framboise Foam" anyway? And what the hell? *Foam doesn't even sound like something that should be on a plate.*

So this book is about food that's big in taste and small in effort. Just great-tasting stuff with no fancy techniques and definitely no over-the-top ingredients—as in everything-comes-from-a-regular supermarket. Cool concept, huh? It's just a bunch of recipes you'll easily be able to make and enjoy.

This all works because I'm not a chef. In fact, up until a couple of years ago, I wasn't even much of a cook. In 2001, I quit a job at a drug-development company to start a travel show on TV. (The fact that I didn't know anything about the TV business is fodder for another book.) This wasn't a cooking show; it was a travel show. Me, a regular guy, would show people that going to places previously considered difficult—wasn't. If I could navigate the non-English-speaking streets and neighborhoods of Tokyo and have a ball doing it, so could anyone. But a month before I was scheduled to leave for Tokyo and Hong Kong to shoot footage, September 11 hit. And though that day changed thousands of other lives much more significantly than mine, I still needed to figure out what to do when I grew up, because I had no job.

So I decided to stick with the "regular-guy-shows-you-how-to-do-something-you're-not-doing" thing, but I would simply change from travel to something else. And that something else became cooking. But, remember, I'm not a chef. My new thing became cooking because, with no job, I was sitting in front of the TV a lot watching people make complicated food, and that drove me crazy. Why couldn't someone just show how easy it can be, so instead of just watching it be made, people could make it themselves? And guess what: that someone turned out to be me.

I shot a demo, sent it out, and the rest, as they say, is culinary history. And now with 8 Emmys and a ton of TV under my belt, here I am with a cookbook. Based on my show's popularity, it was clear other people felt the way I did, and wanted an easier way. The cool part is that I began my whole cooking adventure thinking it was about the recipes, but I now realize it's not. It's about your attitude. This book is only a guide—a good guide, but still only a guide.

You can cook, too, but some of you just don't know it yet.

Sam the Cooking Guy, January 2008

Basic Stuff to Know

Keeping a few concepts in mind and a few basic items around will make your cooking life much easier and ultimately better. So I've put them in three totally-not-sophisticated categories: Thoughts, Food, and Things. And of course there are other things that could be on these lists but aren't. *Hey, I can't cover the whole flippin' world, you know.*

Thoughts

Measuring is a waste of time. Unless you're baking (which is more like a science and requires exact amounts), cooking is like throwing a hand grenade—close is actually good enough. I'll bet if you tried pouring a tablespoon of sugar in your hand right now without a measuring spoon, you'd get pretty darn close, and that would be close enough. If you end up with a little more or a little less butter, a little more or less broth, or whatever, it really won't make a huge difference. But what's really cool is that once you free yourself from measuring, you find freedom in other parts of the kitchen as well. Suddenly you're trying things just because they seem like a good idea, or you're using eggplant when ground beef is called for, because you're confident. Which leads, beautifully, to my next thought . . .

Play the "I don't have that ingredient" game, and force yourself to be creative. We all make the same recipes over and over. If it's Wednesday, it must be Grandma Ruth's chicken. I say the next time you go to the store to buy the ingredients for a tried-and-true (and worn-out) recipe, you should pretend that one of the ingredients no longer exists and force yourself to swap it for something else. A different meat, a different sauce, cheese, stuffing . . . whatever. Change is good, and that's what this is all about—making you a better and more comfortable cook.

Heat is your friend. People don't use enough heat. It's that simple. We all know what properly cooked food should look like—and there are usually two ways to get there: a little heat for a long time, which tends to dry things out (steaks, fish, etc.), or a lot of heat for a little time, which tends to sear the outside and keep the center moist. I put a pan on the heat, let it get hot, and *then* add the oil. Don't be afraid to heat a pan really well before cooking in it. This also applies to your BBQ. Turn the gas grill on, close the lid, and leave it alone for at least 10 minutes. When you come back, it'll be ready for you.

And speaking of heat, I call 350°F the "universal temperature." If you ever forget what you're supposed to cook something at, 350°F will always work—and I'm not kidding here. Oh sure, some things will benefit from a slightly higher or lower temperature if you know it, but don't let it wreck your life if you don't. I've always thought that oven knobs should have just one setting: 350°F. Cooking would be so much easier.

Food

How many times have you stood in front of an open cupboard or fridge wondering what you could make with the seemingly random collection of items in front of you? This whole cooking thing can be made a lot easier by just keeping a few essentials around.

Deli-Roasted Chicken, aka Rotisserie Chicken: This

may be one of the best things in a supermarket these days that is not in the tequila aisle. Here's how I see it: You can buy an uncooked chicken for about five bucks, take it home, unwrap it, remove the bag of "stuff" from inside the bird, rinse it like crazy, being careful not to get the chicken juice everywhere, put it in a roasting pan, rub it with a little butter and a handful of spices, heat up the oven, and cook the bird for an hour and a half until it's done. Or, you can buy a crispy-skinned, juicy, rotisserie-roasted chicken for about a buck more that's ready for many of the recipes in this book. Check out the ingeniously titled chapter Just Chicken (page 102) for a few ideas.

Frozen Shrimp: "Frozen" is not a four-letter word. That's

partly because it has six letters, but also because it can make your life way easier. But when I say "frozen shrimp," I'm not talking about those nasty little curly-pink, already-cooked things in a frozen clump. I'm merely suggesting that a bag of frozen, raw, deveined shell-on shrimp can come in mighty handy. They defrost in a couple of minutes and can be used for a million things, from pizza to stir-fries to chowder (page 69). Frozen shrimp are sold by size. For example, most of the time, I buy 31/40s, which mean there are between thirty-one and forty of them per pound. And since they're frozen, buy them when they're on sale and just stick 'em in the freezer so you have shrimp handy whenever you need it. By the way, you can defrost a bag of shrimp in a large bowl of cool water in about ten minutes.

Tortillas: The "bread of the twenty-first century." At my house, we always have a stack around for quesadillas, wraps, tacos, or anything else we can think of. Turkey and shredded cheese? An amazingly quick quesadilla. Eggs, peppers, and onions? Make a breakfast burrito. Leftover grilled chicken and Caesar salad? Make a Mediterranean wrap. Stuff them with anything you've got, and they're all good. And if you have nothing, just warm one up, brush it with a little butter, and sprinkle with a little salt. Man, oh man.

Prebaked Pizza Crust: Don't be a crust snob. Just go buy a couple and huck 'em in the freezer. "Huck," by the way, is Canadian slang for "throw." Almost any combination of stuff in your fridge will turn a prebaked pizza crust into something great. And, yes, you can do much better than pepperoni and cheese.

"Ready Bacon": Bacon is just one of those things that adds a ton of flavor, and I use it a lot. But I don't use the old-school "make-a-complete-greasy-mess-and-take-forever-to-

cook" type. I use what I call "ready-style" bacon. Looks great, tastes great, is already cooked, and takes only a few seconds to heat. The late-night BLT just went from twenty minutes to five! *Talk about a life-changing food.*

Really Good Olive Oil: Buy yourself a great extra-virgin olive oil (no initials here, I can spell out the actual words) not so much for cooking but rather for "finishing." Just before serving, a good drizzle on the Painless Risotto (page 200),

or on some blue cheese that's been crumbled on top of a steak will make a huge and very good difference. Or even on fresh, ripe tomatoes—a little drizzle of the oil with nothing more than a little kosher salt and some freshly ground black pepper makes the simplest but most amazing little salad. But it's a personal thing, and good oil's not cheap, so try before you buy. Many decent cookware stores will have oil you can sample.

Vermouth: Forget the fact that it's a must-have for any self-respecting martini—you'll be surprised how a splash of vermouth can add tons of flavor to a dish. It's the perfect wine substitute in a recipe, and the fact that it lasts forever means that you don't have to open a new bottle of wine every time you need a quarter of a cup. Next time you make a burger, throw a little vermouth on the mushrooms you're sautéing to go on top. What? You don't sauté mushrooms to go on top of your burgers? Boy, have I got a lot of work to do.

Dried Pasta: Will keep almost forever, and with only a couple of other ingredients, beats the hell out of having toast for dinner—and it's almost as fast. I buy different-shaped pasta to make things interesting. Try the Lemon Pasta with Mint (page 143) with only pasta, butter, mint, and lemon. You'll be glad you read this.

Kosher Salt: Salt should be declassified as a condiment, and moved to its own, much more important, food group. Used properly, it's meant to bring out the natural flavor of

whatever it is you're cooking, not to make things salty. When a recipe calls for you to sprinkle salt on a piece of meat or fish before cooking, you should be using kosher. The grains are big and easy to sprinkle, plus a tablespoon of kosher has less sodium than a tablespoon of regular salt. *And, if a rabbi ever shows up to visit unannounced, you'll have something you can serve.* (Kidding, kidding.)

Freshly Ground Pepper:

Any recipe in this book that calls for pepper will say "freshly ground black pepper." That's because you just can't get the same taste out of that goofy little pepper shaker. I'm not a food snob, but I couldn't live without my grinder. Pepper without a grinder is like Fred without Ginger, sweet without sour, or yin without yang. All you need is a simple grinder and peppercorns. It may be a small thing, but freshly ground pepper is often the only thing you need to finish a dish. Get a grinder and then throw away the sad little shaker.

Things

Let me say right off the bat, I'm not a gadget guy, and I think most gadgets clutter up your drawers and are a horrible waste of money. That having been said, there are definitely some things worth spending money on. There's an old expression about having "the right tool for the job," and this was never truer than in the kitchen. (Except maybe the operating room; the right tool is probably more important there. And on a spaceship, too, I guess.) *Okay*, **let's just say that a few essentials here will make your kitchen life much easier and will make you a better cook. I'll start with the three most important things to me: a knife, tongs, and a wooden cutting board.**

At Least One Good Knife: You probably don't need a whole set of knives, just a decent one or two. Here are a few of my dos and don'ts when shopping for one. Buy what *you* want and not what a salesperson says you need. They'll say you must have a set of this or that, and it's just not true. A good knife can be expensive, and though I have a lot of them, I find myself going back to the same two or three. Find a good-size knife with a handle that's comfortable in your hand, because that's the one you'll use most often. Many people like a chef's knife, not just because it sounds like something worth aspiring to but more for its all-purpose utility. I use a sort of Asian vegetable knife that has a wider blade that's good for scooping, etc. A decent knife will have some heft to both its weight and price. Weight, because the steel should be a little thicker and will go all the way through the handle, and price because good steel and good craftsmanship is just more expensive. Sorry, but it is.

And remember, once you've spent a bunch of money on your new, high-quality knife, you need to take care of it. That means keeping it sharp. Get yourself a "steel," one of those long sharpening things you see the Zorro-like flashy guys using on TV. You don't have to use it like they do, but you do have to use it. Or you could get a "chantry"—it's a pull-through type of sharpener. Not only is a sharp knife hugely important because it makes kitchen life way easier, but it's also safer. As my editor, Justin, likes to remind me: "People don't sharpen their knives, so they need to press a lot harder to do even simple tasks like cutting tomatoes, and they slip because the dull knife can't do the job, or all that extra pressure sends the knife flying." (Apparently he likes long sentences.)

Tongs:
A good pair of tongs will make your whole kitchen time better and easier. A spring-loaded, short-handled model is ideal. Resist the temptation to get one of those long, goofy numbers with no tension. With the right pair, you should be able to pick up something as large and heavy as a salami, as well as something small like a quarter. It's all about control.

Wooden Cutting Board:
It's time to stop worrying about using wood. The reality is that wooden boards are less likely to hold onto bacteria than anything else. But you don't have to take my word for it. According to the study "Disease Determinants of Sporadic Salmonellosis," "Those using wooden cutting boards in their home kitchens were less than half as likely as average to contract salmonellosis;

those using synthetic (plastic or glass) cutting boards were about twice as likely as average to contract salmonellas; and the effect of cleaning the board regularly after preparing meat on it was not statistically significant."

What does this mean? It means you should throw out the plastic and buy wood. And anyone with a glass cutting board should be . . . well, I won't even go there. And do I need to mention that the new knife I've just persuaded you to buy will last a lot longer cutting on wood than anything else?

The Rice Cooker: Asian food is my favorite, and I could have rice at every meal. Gone are the days of nasty, burnt rice in the pot because you forgot it was on the stove. A rice cooker is the only way to make perfect rice every time. You simply put in the rice, add water, turn it on, and walk away. When it's done, it stays warm and perfect for hours. I couldn't live without mine. There are many types, and they range from $25 to $150. But apart from timers and special settings, the $25 models work just as well as the expensive ones. Just get one. I buy Calrose rice for it—a kind of medium-grain rice. It is shorter and stickier and less fluffy than long-grain rice, and it goes with everything. Once you have a rice cooker, check out the Fridge Fried Rice (page 132).

Wok: Buy a cheap wok—or at least one that works. If you have a Teflon-coated wok, I suggest you go get it, take it to the trash, and throw it in—because it's useless. The thing that makes a wok a wok is partially the shape, but also how

it takes and controls a ton of heat. Teflon coatings totally inhibit the heat thing and thus render them basically useless. I have a cheap, fifteen-dollar carbon steel flat-bottom version that I use for a lot of stuff, and wouldn't trade for all the tea in China. (Don't you think the guy who came up with that expression could have found something that maybe more people wanted? Don't get me wrong, I like tea, but all that China has? That's going to be a lot of frickin' tea.)

Some Cool Serving Pieces: This may seem silly,

because it's not like what you serve something on is going to affect the taste, but it could definitely affect the important initial impression, which then could affect the taste. It kills me to think you might make something totally great (like the Warm Cabbage Salad on page 80) and then serve it on your kid's purple plastic Barney plates, with matching cups. It's no coincidence that most restaurants use white to serve on—everything just looks better on white. And don't think I'm telling you to go buy everything new, because I'm not. Just one or two decent, cool serving pieces . . . that's not a lot to ask, is it?

The weekends are very

I Love
Brunch

different from the week-days, right? So **why** make the food the same? Go out on a limb and make something different—and a different cereal doesn't cut it. Unless you mix two or three of them together like my Grandma Jenny used to do. (She was a cereal master. What that woman could do with Cheerios®, Lucky Charms®, and shredded wheat would make your head spin.)

"Three-Two-One" Pomegranate Sammy's Hash Pull-Apart Lox, Spinach, Mush Frittata French Tuna Cristo & Goat Cheese Benedict Banana Toast Blueberry

Bloody Mary
Champagne
Browns Cinnamon
Eggs & Onions
room & Bacon
Toast Mountain
Smoked Salmon
Pizza Pastrami
Bread French
Cinnamon Ring

Liquid Brunch

Nothing says brunch like a "hello" cocktail, and these are two that we serve to kick-start the day. But we don't have them "every day," only on brunch days for God's sake—just days that end in a *y*.

"Three-Two-One" Bloody Mary

Serves 1

This is a hybrid of the Canadian version of a Bloody Mary. It's made with Clamato juice instead of tomato—but don't worry, it's not like drinking a bowl of clams.

Ice
3 ounces vodka
2 ounces Clamato juice *you'll find it in the store by the tomato juice*
1 ounce dark beer (like Newcastle Brown Ale) *—save the rest for a marinade*
2 teaspoons Worcestershire sauce
1 fat teaspoon prepared horseradish
½ teaspoon celery salt
2 or 3 good dashes of your favorite hot sauce
3 good grinds black pepper
1 large wedge of lime

Fill a cocktail shaker ⅓ of the way with ice and also add ice to a serving glass. **Add** the vodka, Clamato, beer, Worcestershire, horseradish, celery salt, hot sauce, and pepper to the shaker. **Shake** really well and pour over the fresh ice in the glass. **Squeeze** and drop in the lime wedge, sit back, and enjoy.

Note: The urge to hum "O Canada" is completely natural and, I assure you, only temporary.

Pomegranate Champagne

Serves 6

I'm not a huge champagne guy, and even less huge when it comes to the classic Mimosa (champagne & OJ), which I find a bit sweet. But pomegranate juice is tart and makes a very different, yet still special drink. There's really no need to buy expensive champagne when you're mixing it like this—that would just be unnecessary.

Ice
One 750 ml bottle of champagne or sparkling wine
by the way, "sparkling wine" is just champagne that comes from somewhere other than the "Champagne" region of France
9 ounces pomegranate juice
1 lemon, cut into wedges

Add ice to glasses, then fill with champagne and juice.
Squeeze, then drop in the lemon wedge and serve.

21

Sammy's Hash Browns

Serves 2

Breakfast is easily my favorite meal, and over the years I'm sure I've had hundreds of pounds of lousy, weak, or tasteless hash browns (which somehow I still managed to eat). But the thought of all those bad extra calories just makes me want to scream. *Learn from my mistakes and make these.*

1 teaspoon olive oil

½ **onion** *any color you like*, **diced small**

½ **red bell pepper, diced small**

Half of a 2-ounce package of "ready bacon,"
   diced small

1 large russet potato, peeled and shredded just
   before you're going to use it

Kosher salt and freshly ground black pepper to taste

Sour cream, for serving (optional)

Heat the olive oil in a nonstick pan over medium heat. Add the onion and red pepper and cook, stirring occasionally, until softened, about 5 minutes. Add the bacon and cook for another couple of minutes. **Squeeze** and discard any liquid from the potato, add to the cooked onion and pepper, and mix well. **Flatten** down with a spatula, and cook until crispy and brown on the bottom. Then **flip** and **cook** until crispy and brown on the other side—you're cooking it like a giant pancake. **Serve** in wedges alone or with some sour cream.

A little inexpensive caviar on the sour cream wouldn't be the worst thing in the world, you know.

Don't Eat the Whole Thing

One question I get asked a lot is "Will you do more low fat, low carb kinda stuff?" And here's my answer: my recipes are already low fat and low carb... if you don't eat the entire thing yourself. When a recipe says "Serves 6," it should. Get it?

Cinnamon
Pull-Apart

Makes 1 Bundt pan's worth

Hot, drippy, gooey, and cinnamon-y—the ideal weekend food. It's also the ideal *"I'm sorry"* peace offering. Plus, it can right a bunch of wrongs. You make it for someone and you're not only saying "I'm sorry" but also "Boy, was it foolish of me to say you're starting to age just like your mother."

1 cup pecan pieces

½ cup raisins

1⅔ cups granulated sugar

1½ sticks (12 tablespoons) butter

2 teaspoons ground cinnamon

Three 10-ounce packages refrigerator biscuits, quartered

Preheat the oven to 350°F. **Grease** a Bundt pan really well and scatter half the pecans and raisins in the bottom. **Stir** 1 cup of the sugar and all the butter in a small pot over medium heat until melted and well combined. Keep on very low heat. **Mix** the cinnamon with the remaining ⅔ cup of sugar in a large bowl. **Drop** half of the biscuit quarters in the bowl of cinny-sugar, a few at a time, to coat them well with the mixture and then put them in the Bundt pan on top of the pecans and raisins. **Drizzle** half the melted butter mixture evenly over the biscuits and top with the remaining pecans and raisins. **Finish** by coating the remaining biscuits with the cinny-sugar, put them in the Bundt pan, and drizzle with the remaining butter. **Bake** for about 40 minutes until golden brown and the top springs back when pushed lightly. **Remove** from the oven and carefully turn upside down on a platter big enough to handle some of the gooey caramel-y stuff running down the sides.

And here's your big moment: you walk over to your loved one with this warm, amazing-looking thing and apologize for whatever you did. If they forgive you, everything's cool and you enjoy the pull-apart together. If they don't, you just walk away, taking the pull-apart with you to eat alone. Seriously, either way it ends pretty good.

I've always thought that brunch had less stress attached to it than any other meal. It's partially the time of day, and partially the attitude—casual clothes, casual food, and what's not to like about morning cocktails?

Lox, Eggs & Onions

Serves 2

Lox—thinly sliced cured salmon—goes **really** well with eggs. Okay, so if you're not Jewish this'll be more in my ethnic camp than yours, but it's a classic and worth trying. And in case you like it so much you think about converting, we just happen to be taking applications right now.

½ tablespoon butter

¼ cup small diced yellow onion

One 4-ounce package lox, chopped fine

4 large eggs, beaten

Kosher salt and freshly ground black pepper to taste *come on, would you expect any other kind of salt in this recipe?* **but go easy on the salt because the lox is already salty.**

Melt the butter in a large nonstick pan over medium heat and cook the onion, stirring occasionally, until it starts to brown *I said "starts"; I didn't say all "becomes burned up,"* about 5 minutes. **Add** the lox to the onion, cook a bit, and allow to heat through. **Pour** in the eggs and cook like scrambled eggs, stirring to break up, until they're done to your liking. I just mean make them as moist or dry as you like. *I don't like mine too dry. . . . Okay, I don't like mine dry at all.*

Spinach, Mushroom & Bacon Frittata

Serves 8

Don't shy away from brunch because you think you have to stand in the kitchen and make 75 poached eggs and a jillion pancakes. This easy frittata throws together in no time, requires no baby-sitting, and still rules the day—make that the next day . . . it may even be **better** the next day.

One 10-ounce package frozen chopped spinach, defrosted

10 large eggs, beaten

1 tablespoon olive oil

2 cloves garlic, chopped fine

1 red bell pepper, diced small

8 ounces sliced white mushrooms

One 2-ounce package "ready bacon"

One 6-ounce bag baby spinach

3/4 cup freshly-shredded Parmesan cheese
(not the powdered kind)

Kosher salt and freshly ground black pepper to taste

Sour cream, for serving (optional)

Salsa, for serving (optional)

Preheat the oven to 400°F. Squeeze and drain the spinach of as much water as possible. Put in a large bowl with the eggs and set aside. Heat a large-ish pan over medium heat and add the oil, garlic, red pepper and mushrooms. **Cook**, stirring occasionally, until the pepper and mushrooms have softened, about 10 minutes. **Toss** in the bacon and cook, stirring occasionally, until it has gotten a little crispy. **Dump** the fresh spinach on top and stir in until it's wilted way down. **Add** the mushroom-bacon mixture to the eggs with ½ cup of Parmesan and the salt and pepper, and mix well. **Pour** into a buttered 9 × 9–inch casserole dish and top with the remaining Parmesan. **Bake** until fully set, about 25 minutes. **Slice** and serve with a dollop *what a stupid word* of sour cream and a splash *hey, I needed something equally dumb* of salsa, if desired.

Salted vs. Unsalted Butter

I know the chef-type people tend to make an issue of using unsalted butter. I don't, but then I'm not a chef. I've never used unsalted butter for anything and won't start now. I taste, I season, and I'm aware of what I put into things. Plus, I don't want to have to deal with buying two types of butter, and I certainly don't want to end up using unsalted butter on my toast instead of regular—that would blow.

French Toast Mountain

Serves 2

I made this one day when my kids were little and they still ask for it today. Everyone likes it. Everyone except for **Mrs.** Cooking Guy, that is—she just eats fruit in the morning. Can you say b-o-r-i-n-g?

2 large eggs, beaten in a large bowl

1 tablespoon granulated sugar

1 teaspoon cinnamon

2 tablespoons milk

2 tablespoons butter

5 slices bread—*white, wheat, whatever*

Syrup

Powdered sugar

Beat the eggs with the sugar and cinnamon and stir in the milk. **Preheat** a nonstick pan or griddle over medium heat. Add the butter and spread it around. **Working** with however many bread slices will fit in the pan or griddle, dip the bread in the egg mess and transfer to the pan to cook *so far just like regular French toast, right?* **Cook** until golden-y brown and beginning to get just very slightly crispy around the edges, then turn and cook the same way on the other side. **Remove** from the heat, cut the bread into 1-inch squares, and place in a mountain-like pile on two plates. Drizzle with syrup first; this would be the "cascading waterfall" part of the mountain. Then dust the top of the pile with powdered sugar; this gives it the "snowy peaks" part of the mountain. *Okay, so I like to play with my food. What's the big deal?*

Quick Cooking

I've officially had it up to here with the "quick-food" craze. A trip through the supermarket these days will reveal a million "no-need-to-cook" items in every category imaginable. It's not even cooking anymore, its just opening. "Come on kids, it's time for packages!" I'm just waiting for the day when they sell a premade dinner shrink-wrapped with the guy to open it for you. My real fear is that we're slowly breeding out the cooking gene and in twenty years it will be all but forgotten. Picture the astronauts with their little packages of squeeze food, because that'll be us. "Grandma, what was cooking?" "Well, dear, that was something we used to do before we knew better. Now, who wants another tube of meat loaf?"

Tuna Cristo

This is the way-less-sophisticated cousin of the classic "Monte Cristo," which is made with ham, chicken, and Gruyère cheese—but I honestly think mine is easily as good and a heck of a lot easier 'cuz you've always got tuna in the cupboard. *You've always got tuna in the cupboard, right?*

One 6-ounce can tuna, drained well *I like the packed-in-water kind*

2 tablespoons finely diced red bell pepper

2 tablespoons mayo

Kosher salt and freshly ground black pepper to taste

4 slices bread

2 slices cheese *provolone or fontina is great here*

2 tablespoons butter

2 large eggs, beaten

In a bowl, mix the tuna, red pepper, mayo, and salt and pepper well. Spread the mixture evenly on 2 of the bread slices, add a slice of cheese on one of the bread slices, and top with the second slice of bread. Repeat with the remaining bread slices. *I realize this may be really obvious, but trust me, there'll always be a person who wonders what to do with the remaining slices of bread.*

Preheat a nonstick pan over medium heat, add the butter, and swirl it around. **Dip** each sandwich in the beaten eggs like you're making French toast. **Cook** the sandwiches until golden brown. **Turn** and **cook** on the other side until the cheese is melted. **Serve** warm *probably also not necessary, but why stop now, right?*

They (whoever they are) make a microwave egg poacher. Is it me, or is there just something wrong with the idea of microwaved eggs?

Smoked Salmon & Goat Cheese Pizza

Makes one 12-inch pizza

I don't want you thinking I use lox a lot because I'm Jewish and we make some sort of commission on it (the commission's on the kosher salt). It's that lox just screams brunch or breakfast to me—so bring it on.

5 ounces goat cheese, softened

One 12-inch prebaked pizza crust *go thin if you have a choice, or not—I mean, who am I to dictate what kind of crust you use?*

3 tablespoons finely chopped fresh dill

½ small red onion, thinly sliced

One 4-ounce package lox

3 tablespoons small capers, drained (optional)

Preheat the oven to 425°F. **Spread** the goat cheese over the crust, sprinkle with half the dill, and then top with the onion. **Bake** until the crust starts getting crispy, about 12 minutes. **Remove** from the oven, top with the lox, the remaining dill, and the capers *if you're so inclined, which you should be*.

Slice into wedges and serve.

Pastrami Benedict

Makes 4 Bennys

Let me put it this way: if an order of regular eggs Benedict is like a pretty, delicate woman—my version is like her 250-pound Harley-riding older brother Gus. I like Gus, and so will you.

1 cup beef gravy *no need to make it— you can buy it at the store*

1 tablespoon prepared horseradish

4 large eggs

6 ounces thinly sliced pastrami

2 English muffins, split

Freshly ground black pepper (optional)

Mix the gravy and horseradish together in a small pot and warm over lowish heat. **Poach** the eggs (see Note). While the eggs poach, **grill** the pastrami on both sides in a nonstick pan over medium heat. While the eggs poach and the pastrami grills, **toast** the muffins. *You're seeing that there's a process and order here, right?*

Build it like this:

Place grilled pastrami on each toasted English muffin, top with an egg, and spoon horseradish gravy over the top. A little freshly ground black **pepper** would be a good thing right now, and you're done. *Holy crap.*

Note: This is not meant to be Poached Egg 101, but here are two options: I go unsophisticated with a small metal ramekin (about ½ cup in size), which I butter well, crack an egg into, and put in a covered pan of gently boiling water that comes about halfway up the side of the ramekin. About 2 minutes later you need to watch the time the white is set and the yolk is still soft—beautiful. The other option is to quickly stir a cracked egg into a swirling pot of rapidly boiling water—but that always ends for me in a creepy, stringy, and completely un-servable egg mess. But you decide.

You can pass off almost anything

as brunch food—that's the beauty of it. Lasagna, sandwiches, salads, last night's roast beef, and of course eggs—what a great concept!

Banana Bread French Toast

Serves 4 *or 2 if you eat it like I do*

This is one of the fanciest store-bought things you'll ever make. Oh sure, you can make your own banana bread from scratch, but why bother? I either buy a mix or a loaf already baked. My vote is for the mix; that way you've always got it. Keep a box in the pantry and make it the night before.

3 large eggs

3 tablespoons milk

2 tablespoons Grand Marnier

1 tablespoon sugar

2 tablespoons butter

Eight 1-inch-thick slices of banana bread

¼ cup maple syrup, warmed

Beat the eggs in a flat bowl. **Stir** in the milk, Grand Marnier, and sugar. **Melt** the butter in a nonstick pan over medium heat. **Dip** the bread slices in the egg mixture and cook until golden-y brown on the bottom. **Turn** and cook on the other side. **Serve** with the maple syrup.

Note: Once, in an emergency, I purchased banana bread slices from a gas station market, and it was still really, really good.

Blueberry Cinnamon Ring

Serves 8

I love those little refrigerator biscuits. They can come in handy for a ton of things. Made with frozen blueberries, this crazy ring kills.

2 tablespoons butter

½ cup frozen blueberries—*the baby guys, if you can find them*

1 tablespoon cinnamon

½ cup sugar

Two 10-ounce cans (24 count) refrigerator biscuits *seriously*

Preheat the oven to 375°F. **Butter** a Bundt pan really well. **Place** about half of the berries on the bottom of the pan. **Mix** the cinnamon and sugar together in a bowl. **Separate** the biscuits and dip in the sugar mixture. **Place** the sugar-coated biscuits flat side beside flat side in the bottom of the pan, until a full circle of them is completed. **Put** the remaining berries on top and push some of them in between the biscuits. **Bake** until brown and firmish to the touch, about 30 minutes. **Loosen** the edges carefully, turn upside down on a large platter, and serve.

This is my favorite way to

Appetizers

eat—a little bit of a lot of things. It's like I have FADD, Food Attention Deficit Disorder. In a restaurant, I get bored with one thing and find myself looking at the plates of the people I'm with. "Can I try that? Is that good? **Wow**, they really gave you a lot of scallops." I can be totally annoying, so I go with three or four appetizers. Everyone's better off for it.

Pesto Pizza Salt
Honey Garlic
Bread Gooey Blue
Onion Quesadillas
Goat Cheese Mini
Sandwiches
Pie "Whatever"
Artichoke-y Red
Chunky Guacamole
Devilled Eggs
Won Ton Chips

and Pepper Shrimp
Spareribs Garlic
Cheese and Red
Bruschetta with
Crab Cake
One Dank Tomato
Spring Rolls
Pepper Dip Sam's
Smoked Salmon
Sausage Rolls
Toasted Pitas

Pesto **Pizza**

This is one of our standbys at my house—something we make all the time because people love it and it's a snap. It's also the perfect thing to take to someone's home as an appetizer. You can make it at your house and bake it at theirs. You can even buy the four ingredients on the way to their place and make the whole thing there.

One 4-ounce garlic-and-herb soft, spreadable cheese *I use Alouette®*
One 12-inch ready-made pizza crust
3 ounces ready-made pesto
2 ounces Parmesan cheese, grated (about ¼ cup)

Preheat the oven to 425°F. **Spread** the garlic-and-herb cheese over the crust. **Spread** the pesto evenly over the top of the cheese. **Sprinkle** the Parmesan cheese over the top of the pesto. **Bake** until the top starts to get bubbly and the crust a little brown, 10 to 12 minutes. **Slice** into thin wedges and serve.

Salt and Pepper Shrimp

Serves 6 for an appetizer

You know those "ready-to-go" cocktail shrimp platters they sell at the supermarket? The ones filled with pink, precooked shrimp on a bed of some weird lettuce-y thing, with a container of weak cocktail sauce in the middle? These are nothing like those. Make them at the last minute in front of your guests—they're kind of impressive. Part of the fun is having to peel them first.

½ tablespoon kosher salt

½ tablespoon freshly ground black pepper

1 tablespoon peanut oil

2 large cloves garlic, chopped fine

½-inch piece of fresh ginger, peeled and chopped fine

1 bunch green onions (scallions), white and light green parts only, cut into 2-inch lengths

1 pound large raw shrimp *the 31/40s are the perfect size; use the shell-on, deveined, easy-peel type, but do not peel them*

In a small bowl, mix the salt and pepper together and set aside. Turn on the fan above your stove, heat a wok or pan until really, really hot and smoking, and then add the oil. Wait until the pan begins to smoke even more, then add the garlic, ginger, green onions, and shrimp. **Stir** often until the shrimp are almost fully cooked, which should not take more than a couple of minutes. Then **add** the salt and pepper. **Stir** quickly to coat all of the shrimp in the salt and pepper mixture. **Remove** from the pan and serve (with a small bowl for the shells).

Note: *Since these are ideally made in a wok, this would be the perfect time to review my thinking about woks in Basic Stuff to Know, page 13.*

Remember that hollowed-out
loaf of sourdough bread that was filled with spinach dip...from like the 60s? It belongs there.

Honey Garlic Spareribs

Serves 6 as an appetizer

This is a standard guest appetizer in the Cooking Guy household. Why? How about because these fantastic-looking sticky ribs are totally loved by everyone who has them? Plus, when your guests come over, *your house smells unbelievable*. But because they're ribs, they'll need a little pre-cooking, which you can always do the day before if you want. Just make sure they're at room temp for the final cooking phase.

About 4 to 5 pounds of pork back spareribs (2 racks)

2 tablespoons garlic powder

3/4 cup soy sauce

3/4 cup honey

2 tablespoons cider vinegar

3 cloves garlic, crushed

1/2 teaspoon freshly ground black pepper

4 green onions (scallions), white and light green parts only, thinly sliced

1 teaspoon sesame seeds

Preheat the oven to 350°F. **Cut** the racks into individual ribs and season with the garlic powder. **Arrange** the ribs in a single layer in a baking dish and cover tightly with foil. **Bake** until very tender, about 1 hour. While they bake, go think about who you want to invite over because these are definitely worth sharing. **Combine** the soy sauce, honey, vinegar, crushed garlic, and pepper in a saucepan and simmer over medium-low heat for about 5 minutes. **Remove** the ribs from the oven and drain them well. *Be careful—there will be lots of steam.* **Pour** the soy-honey mixture over the ribs, making sure they are well coated. **Return** to the oven and bake, uncovered, for about another hour, basting well about every 10 minutes. **Remove** from the oven and put them on that cool-looking platter I told you to buy (see Basic Stuff to Know, page 15). **Garnish** the top with the green onions and sesame seeds, and serve.

Cooking for Guests

An e-mail from a viewer: "Dear Sam, we had some special guests over recently, and I wanted to make something very special to serve. I tried something new that just didn't work out." Then I was asked for my advice on the seasoning and cooking of the dish—where did she go wrong, she wondered. I told her she went wrong by trying to make something for the first time for guests. Why try something you've never made when you want to impress? I wouldn't. I told her that next time they either make something they're very comfortable with, or if they must try a new dish, make it a really easy one, like one of mine.

Garlic Bread

Makes 1 baguette's worth—about 20 pieces

This is great garlic bread. That foil-bag thing in the supermarket that says "garlic bread" on it is not good (in fact it's barely garlic bread). Oh sure, they want you to think it's good, but trust me, it's not.

8 tablespoons (1 stick) butter, at room temperature

¾ cup shredded Parmesan cheese *which means* **not powdered;** *either buy it already grated or use a grater*

⅓ cup finely chopped fresh Italian parsley *the flat kind*

4 big cloves garlic, chopped fine

1 teaspoon red pepper flakes

1 long sourdough baguette, cut down the middle lengthwise

Preheat the broiler. In a small bowl, **combine** the butter, ½ cup of the Parmesan, the parsley, garlic, and red pepper flakes; mix well. **Spread** the cheese mixture on the cut sides of the bread. Sprinkle the top with the remaining ¼ cup Parmesan cheese. **Place** on a baking sheet and put under the broiler, but not too close. **Broil** until the bread begins to get brown and crispy. **Remove** from the oven, slice into 2-inch pieces, and serve *making fun of that supermarket stuff while you do.*

Gooey Blue Cheese and Red Onion Quesadillas

Serves 6 to 8 as an appetizer

Think about this: warm, gooey blue cheese with red onion that's been caramelized with brown sugar. On second thought, don't think about it. Just make it. In fact, I think I'll go make it right now.

1 red onion, thinly sliced

¹/₂ tablespoon olive oil

1 tablespoon brown sugar

2 ounces blue cheese, crumbled

8 corn tortillas, about 5 inches round *did I need to say* round? *I mean, have you ever seen a square tortilla?*

In a medium nonstick pan, **cook** the onion in olive oil over medium heat, stirring, until it becomes very soft, about 10 minutes. Add the brown sugar and mix well. **Add** the blue cheese and keep on heating and stirring until the cheese melts. **Remove** the pan from the heat, divide the onion and blue cheese mixture, and spread onto 4 of the tortillas. **Top** each one with another tortilla. **Wipe** out the pan and cook each quesadilla until lightly browned on both sides. **Remove** from the pan and allow them to cool slightly. Cut into wedges and serve.

Bruschetta with Goat Cheese

Makes approximately 20 pieces

Whether you pronounce this "broo-SHETTA" or "broo-SKETTA," the genius is the addition of the goat cheese. It makes the basic little broo totally great.

1½ pounds ripe tomatoes, seeded, then diced small

3 large cloves garlic, chopped fine

10 large fresh basil leaves, coarsely chopped

1 teaspoon fresh lemon juice

2 tablespoons olive oil

Kosher salt and freshly ground black pepper to taste

4 ounces goat cheese, softened

1 baguette, cut lengthwise

Preheat the broiler. In a bowl, **mix** together the tomatoes, garlic, basil, lemon juice, olive oil, salt, and pepper. **Spread** the goat cheese on the sliced baguette. Top with the tomato mixture. Put on a baking sheet and **place** under the broiler, but not too close, until beginning to brown nicely, 1 to 2 minutes. **Make** sure it doesn't burn. **Remove** from the oven, slice into 2-inch pieces, and serve.

Mini **Crab Cake Sandwiches**

Makes 16 little sandwiches *or 1 huge one (kidding, kidding!)*

Two things have always bugged me about most crab cakes: they're fried in a bunch of oil, and they almost always have a ton of mayo in them. Mine are baked, not fried, and they have zero mayo. Plus these are easy to throw together, easy to cook, and even easier to eat. ***Who loves ya, baby?***

16 refrigerator buttermilk biscuits *(the small size)*

One 8-ounce bag ready-mixed coleslaw (with the dressing included)

1 pound crabmeat (see Note)

⅓ cup panko crumbs (Japanese bread crumbs available at most supermarkets)

¼ cup small-diced green onions (scallions), both green and white parts

3 tablespoons soy sauce

1 to 2 tablespoons Asian chili sauce *not the ketchup-y kind* **(also available at most supermarkets)**

Bake the biscuits and prepare the coleslaw according to the package directions. Set aside the biscuits and put the coleslaw in the fridge. **Preheat** the oven to 400°F. In a bowl, **mix** together the crabmeat, panko, green onions, soy sauce, and chili sauce. **Shape** the mixture into 16 tight little patties and place them on a greased baking sheet. **Bake** the patties until crispy brown on top, 10 to 15 minutes. Flip over carefully and bake until equally crispy brown on the other side. **Cut** the biscuits in half and place one crab cake on each bottom half. Add some coleslaw, then top with the other biscuit half and serve.

Note: When it comes to crabmeat, there's good canned and bad canned. The bad canned comes in a little tin, like tuna. (And if it's spelled with a K, it's junk and fake.) The good canned is in a way-larger can and refrigerated. Ask your seafood guy (that's why they're there), or look for the Phillips brand.

Tasting

Start tasting as you cook. One question I get all the time is how do you know if it's done, or salty, or spicy or...? Taste as you go, that's how. Unless you're a culinary freak of nature like my Grandma Ruth who made the world's best chopped liver and never, ever tasted it, you should be trying things as they are cooking. That way you can correct a problem before it's too late. There's nothing worse than getting a dish to the table only to find out it's gone horribly wrong.

One Dank Tomato Pie

Serves 6 to 8 as an appetizer

This is no quiche—not that there's anything wrong with that. It's just a great collection of simple ingredients that go together really well.

My oldest Max had friends over one day when I was making it, and they ate it—all of it. Here are their exact quotes:

  Nick: Sam, at the top of his game.

  John: It was a loped-out dank piece of pie.

  Dean: It was a gnarly chill pie.

  Josh: It's a creeped-out danky piece of dank cheese pie.

You can see how moved they were. Maybe you should try it for yourself. By the way, "dank" is good.

1 tablespoon olive oil

3 red onions, thinly sliced

Kosher salt and freshly ground black pepper to taste

One 9-inch ready-made unbaked pie crust

1 pound large ripe tomatoes (3 to 4), cut in ¼-inch slices

6 ounces goat cheese with herbs, crumbled

Preheat the oven to 350°F. In a large nonstick pan, add the oil and onions, and season with salt and pepper. **Cook**, stirring, over medium heat until they've shrunk way down and are really well softened, about 15 minutes. **Place** the pie crust in a pie plate and fill with the cooked onions. **Cover** the onions with the tomato slices, placing them in a circular pattern. **Spread** the goat cheese crumbles over the top. **Bake** until the edges become brown, about 20 minutes. **Remove** from the oven, let cool slightly, slice into wedges, and enjoy its dankness.

Note: *This easily makes a main-dish sorta thing. Just serve it with a good salad or soup. It also totally makes the cut as an appetizer. Just serve it on those tiny appetizer plates.*

New Foods

Try new foods at least once.

Imagine you're on your deathbed and decide to try a fish taco for the first time, and you love it. It would suck knowing you'd missed out on hundreds, probably thousands of the delicious little guys over the years, wouldn't it? And just because you've always hated something doesn't mean you always will—taste buds change. I used to despise cilantro and now I can't live without it. So try something new and often. A taste, a little bite, or even just a nibble. You'll be amazed at what you've been missing.

"Whatever" Spring Rolls

Makes 10 rolls

Once you know how easy it is to use the supermarket's readily available spring roll wrappers, you can make these rolls with "whatever" you want: chicken, crab, lobster, or just vegetables. You're totally in the driver's seat.

1 tablespoon peanut oil, plus a little extra for brushing

4 ounces bagged ready mixed coleslaw *the tri-colored kind, without the dressing*

8 ounces "whatever": cooked chicken that's been shredded, crabmeat, chili *it's up to you (okay, maybe not the chili)*

3 tablespoons of your favorite spicy Asian stir-fry sauce, plus extra for dipping

10 large spring roll wrappers

White and black sesame seeds *or just one type, if you can't find both*

Preheat the oven to 375°F. **Heat** a wok until it's almost smoking, then add the oil. **Add** the coleslaw and "whatever" and stir-fry until the slaw is slightly wilted, about 1 minute. **Stir** in the sauce and remove from the heat. Allow to cool

slightly. **Place** one wrapper on the counter with a corner pointing at you. **Put** approximately 2 tablespoons of the filling in the center of the wrapper. **Fold** the nearest corner of the wrapper up, covering the filling. Fold in the two sides and finish by rolling the wrapper away from you. **Moisten** the very end with a dab of water to help it stick and hold the whole thing closed. **Brush** the tops very lightly with oil. Sprinkle with the sesame seeds. **Bake** at 375°F until lightly browned. Cut on the diagonal and serve with extra sauce for dipping.

Artichoke-y Red Pepper Dip

Makes about 3 cups

Almost all of this can come out of your cupboard. Just buy the ingredients, keep 'em on the shelf, and you're golden the next time the in-laws come over. Hold that thought—*maybe you shouldn't make something this good; they might want to come over all the time...*

½ jar roasted red peppers, drained and coarsely chopped (about 6 ounces)

One 14-ounce can artichoke bottoms, drained and coarsely chopped

1 cup shredded Monterey Jack cheese

3 cloves garlic, chopped fine

1 tablespoon fresh lemon juice

½ teaspoon cayenne pepper

3 tablespoons grated Parmesan cheese, *not the powdered kind*

Preheat the oven to 400°F. In a bowl, **mix** together the red peppers, artichokes, cheese, garlic, lemon juice, and cayenne. **Transfer** the mixture to two or three small ovenproof bowls suitable for serving, and sprinkle the Parmesan on top. **Bake** until heated through, bubbly, and delicious, about 20 minutes. **Serve** with toasted pita bread or Won Ton Chips (page 62).

Sam's Chunky Guacamole

Makes about 3 cups

There's guacamole, and then there's **guacamole**, know what I mean? And there's no magic to this. But I do want you to keep the "chunky" part in mind. Please don't mush it out. *And it totally beats the pants off that store-bought crap. I mean "stuff"...no, I mean "crap."*

4 ripe avocados

1 ripe, medium-sized tomato, seeded and diced small

½ cup small-diced white onion *I'm usually not too anal about onions but in this case white is the way to go as it has more bite*

Juice from 1 lime

1 canned chipotle chile, chopped fine *just one, not "I can"*

⅓ cup finely chopped cilantro

Kosher salt to taste

Cut the avocados in half lengthwise and remove the pits. With a large spoon, scoop out the flesh *what else do you call it?* into a bowl and mash it up a bit *I said "a bit," not into soup*. Add the tomato, onion, lime juice, chipotle, and cilantro and blend everything together into a beautifully chunky mixture. Season the guacamole with salt. What are you waiting for? Start eating. Serve with chips, seafood, on a burger, in a sandwich—basically everywhere.

Smoked Salmon Devilled Eggs

Makes 24 halves

If you're thinking devilled eggs belong only on *Leave It to Beaver*, think again. They totally fit into contemporary life, but don't make them only for a party; try them when there are just a couple of you. Just don't eat them all yourself.

12 hard-boiled eggs

One 4-ounce package smoked salmon, chopped fine *here we go with the lox thing again*

⅓ cup mayo

¼ cup small-diced red onion

1 to 2 tablespoons hot sauce, to taste

1 tablespoon spicy brown mustard

Kosher salt and freshly ground black pepper to taste

2 tablespoons caviar (see Note)

2 tablespoons finely chopped green onions (scallions), white and light green parts only

Peel the eggs, then slice them in half lengthwise *(you knew that, right?)*. Put the white halves on a serving plate and the yolks into a bowl. To the yolks, **add** the salmon, mayo, onion, hot sauce, mustard, and salt and pepper. **Mix** well, then fill each of the white halves with the yolk mixture. **Try** this: fill a resealable zipper-top plastic bag with the egg mixture and cut off one of the corners. Then squeeze the mixture out of the hole and fill each egg white like a pro. **Add** a tiny amount of caviar to the top of each egg **just** before serving, then sprinkle with green onions and serve. *You're gonna love these. "Wally, Beaver! Would you come down here please?"*

Note: *This is not the time to go big with the caviar—I mean as in "expensive." Save that for another day. A simple little jar from the supermarket will supply all the salty bite this appetizer needs.*

Cook with Your Kids

We teach our kids so many things, why not how to cook? Years are spent learning tons of stuff we'll barely ever use— calculus comes to mind. In some areas, younger kids are schooled in the art of formal dancing, white gloves on the ladies and the young man with his hand on the small of the young woman's back. In fact the Boy Scouts still teach how to start a fire from nothing. The only time I've ever needed to start a fire from nothing was, oh yes... never.

So why not something they can really use, like cooking? It's at least as important as calculus, formal dancing, and fires—and a hell of a lot more practical.

Sausage Rolls

Makes 24 mini rolls

Too simple? Perhaps. Not fancy enough? Probably. Delicious? You bet your sweet sausage roll they are. These little snacks have been pleasing the Brits for centuries, so who are we to argue? You just buy the puff pastry frozen from the supermarket.

1 frozen puff pastry sheet (from a package of 2)

One 14-ounce package turkey or pork breakfast sausage *the uncooked type, about 14 links*

Approximately ¼ cup flour

Water

½ cup steak sauce

2 tablespoons apricot jam

Let the pastry sheet **defrost** on the counter for about 20 minutes before using. **Preheat** the oven to 350°F. You need to **remove** the sausage casings while maintaining the shape of the sausage, so make a small slice down the length of each sausage, peel off the thin protective casing, and throw it away. *I realize a few of you will consider this a "yucky" step; then maybe it would be best to have someone else do it. (Kids love doing it.)* The pastry sheets come folded in three sections, which are ideal for our purposes. Just use a knife to **cut** the sections apart along the fold lines, and lay one on a floured work surface in front of you. Take a fork and **poke** all over the surface of each sheet to prevent them from ''puffing'' too much. **Place** 3 casing-free sausages end to end lengthwise down the middle of a pastry sheet section. **Roll** the sheet over the sausages, making a long, snug tube. **Moisten** the edge of the pastry with water to help seal it and cut off any excess along the sealed edge. **Cut** each tube into 8 pieces and place the sealed side down on a lightly greased baking sheet. **Repeat** the rolling and cutting process with the remaining pastry and sausages. **Bake** until lightly browned, 20 to 25 minutes. In a small bowl, **mix** the steak sauce and jam, and serve as a dipping sauce. *Go on, mate, have a wee taste. You'll bleedin' love it.*

Condiments Rule

And I just don't mean mustard and mayo—though they both definitely have their place. I just opened my fridge and saw my large collection of random bottles and jars... capers, roasted peppers, kiwifruit hot sauce from New Zealand, horseradish (creamed & prepared), pickled green beans and baby tomatoes for cocktails, chili paste (seeds) & chili sauce (no seeds), and a huge variety of Asian sauces (see the Black Bean Salmon on page 127). Anyway, you get the idea. The point is that all these things can add beautifully to a number of recipes, plus just having them means you might experiment with them.

**It's time to lose the crackers in your cupboard.
We're not six years old anymore.**

Won Ton Chips

Makes as many as you want

These are perfect to use when you have a flavorful dip you don't want to add additional cracker taste to.

Won ton wrappers *round or square 3- to 4-inch; usually sold in the supermarket's produce aisle, in the refrigerated section*

Preheat the oven to 350°F. **Place** individual wrappers on an ungreased baking sheet. **Bake** until just ever so slightly beginning to brown, about 8 minutes. **Remove** from the oven, let cool, and use for dipping as you would any store-bought cracker or chip.

Messy Stuff With

Variety in Beer

Ever been to a party and the host had just one kind of beer? I hate that, and I don't want that to be you. No one would expect you to have a huge variety of vodkas or tequilas. (I do, but that's just me.) But beer? It's really no more expensive to have 3 or 4 different kinds. Just do it.

Toasted Pitas

Makes as many as you want

These things are perfect for serving with appetizers, dips, and spread-kind-of-things.

Pita bread rounds
Butter, softened

Preheat the broiler. **Split** each pita so you end up with two circular halves. Butter the inside of each half lightly and cut into wedges. **Put** on a baking sheet and broil until slightly golden. **Remove** from the oven and serve warm with whatever. *In fact, My Mom's Lox Dip on page 142 is ideal with this.*

This chapter should not

Soup & Salad

be quickly dismissed as some namby-pamby space-taker-upper. The recipes here—the Potato Soup, the Warm Cabbage Salad, the Roasted Tomato and Goat Cheese Salad—are things we often have as complete dinners. **OK**, so maybe we throw a couple of really cold beers in with them, but still . . .

Tortilla Soup Shrimp
Roasted Red
Drop Soup Potato
and Noodle Soup
Blackened Corn
and Tomato Salad
Salad Roasted
Cheese Salad
You Could Ever Do

and Corn Chowder
Pepper Soup Egg
Soup Filipino Pork
French Onion Soup
Salad Green Bean
Warm Cabbage
Tomato and Goat
The Easiest Thing
to a Fruit Salad

Tortilla Soup

This soup is made with jarred salsa, and is all good—which makes it sound like some of my other recipes are all bad, and that's not true. I just mean this is extra good. Okay, I'll stop now.

One 16-ounce jar red salsa, medium hot

2 cups chicken broth

2 cups shredded cooked chicken

Vegetable oil

3 flour tortillas, about 8 inches in diameter

1 ripe avocado, diced small

2 tablespoons finely chopped fresh cilantro

Heat the salsa and broth in a pot on the stove over medium heat. Once it starts to bubble, **add** the shredded chicken and **simmer** until it's all heated through, about 5 minutes. While the soup is warming, **heat** a nonstick pan with about ½ teaspoon of the oil over medium heat and add one of the tortillas. **Cook** until it starts to get a little crispy and brown on each side. **Remove**, cut in half, and then into thin strips. **Repeat** with the other tortillas. **Serve** by putting some soup in a bowl and topping it with some tortilla strips, avocado, and chopped cilantro.

Shrimp and Corn Chowder

Serves 6

I call this a "cheat recipe," but it's one you can learn from, because once you know how quickly a handful of raw shrimp will cook in a soup, you'll be throwing them into all kinds of things.

⅓ cup diced red bell pepper

1 teaspoon olive oil

Two 18-ounce cans of any corn chowder

¾ pound raw shrimp, peeled and deveined
once again I'd go with 31/40s

Hot sauce to taste (optional) *strike that. I don't mean "optional"; I want you to use it*

3 tablespoons finely chopped fresh cilantro

In a nonstick skillet, **cook** the pepper in the oil over medium-high heat until softened but still a little bit crispy, about 5 minutes. **Heat** the chowder in a pot on medium-low heat until simmering. **Add** the shrimp and heat until they're cooked through and opaque, about 5 minutes. **Serve** with a good drizzle of hot sauce to taste and top with the red pepper and cilantro.

Roasted Red Pepper Soup

Serves 6

This soup kills, hot or cold. Feel free to make it using fresh red peppers and going through the whole roasting . . . steaming . . . peeling . . . coring . . . cleaning . . . chopping process; it'll take about an hour. Or you could be done in about 3 minutes by using a jar of the already roasted peppers. But who am I to get in the way?

Two 15-ounce jars roasted red peppers

½ cup yellow onion, diced

2 cloves garlic, chopped fine

1 tablespoon olive oil

1 teaspoon cayenne pepper

3 cups chicken broth

Kosher salt and freshly ground black pepper to taste

For garnish

Sour cream

Fresh cilantro, chopped fine

Drain the peppers well in a colander. In a large pot, **cook** the onion and garlic in the olive oil over medium heat, stirring, until softened, about 5 minutes. **Add** the red peppers and cayenne to the onion and mix well. Put the pepper mixture in a food processor or blender with a cup of the chicken broth and **process** until smooth, about 1 minute. Put the processed mixture back into the pot and **add** the remaining chicken broth. **Season** to taste with the salt and pepper. **Simmer** on low heat for 10 minutes. **Serve** in bowls with a fat spoonful of sour cream, some cilantro, and freshly ground pepper.

Egg Drop Soup

Serves 4

This is Mrs. Cooking Guy's absolutely favorite soup. Instant and simple comfort. If you wanted to go bigger with this, you could always add a little cooked chicken or some veggies. Or to go really big, you could go out and order it in a Chinese restaurant—but that would be kinda nuts because it's so simple to make at home.

4 cups chicken broth

1 large egg

2 tablespoons soy sauce

4 tablespoons thinly sliced green onions (scallions), white and light green parts only, for garnish

Heat the broth in a small pot over medium-high heat and bring to a boil. **Beat** the egg in a small bowl and set aside. When the broth comes to a boil, **add** the soy sauce and let it come to a boil again. Here comes the "drop" part: turn off the heat and while stirring the soup with a fork in a fast, circular motion, slowly **pour** the egg in a thin stream and stir until it gets all cool and kind of stringy-looking. *And that's it.* **Serve** in a bowl with the green onions on top. *Technically, this should probably be called Egg Poured Soup, but it doesn't sound nearly as good.*

Potato Soup

Serves 6

This is one of the best soups ever. It's a party in a bowl—fairly basic, but when you put a whole bunch of other stuff in it, the party takes shape. It's the perfect big-group food because your guests get to work on it themselves, and you just chill.

2 big baking potatoes, peeled and cut into ½-inch cubes *the potatoes need to be cut into equal-size cubes so they cook evenly*

3 cups chicken broth

2 red onions, diced small

2 tablespoons butter

1 teaspoon cayenne, to taste

1½ cups heavy whipping cream

3 tablespoons finely chopped fresh Italian parsley *the flat kind*

Kosher salt and freshly ground black pepper to taste

Put the potatoes and broth in a large pot over medium-high heat, cover, bring just to a boil, then reduce the heat and simmer until the potatoes get soft, about 15 minutes. While that's happening, in a separate nonstick pan, **cook** the onions in the butter with the cayenne, stirring, until softened, about 10 minutes. Then **add** the cooked onions, the whipping cream, and parsley to the soup. While the soup simmers, **mash** some of the potatoes in the pot with the back of a large spoon. This will help the soup thicken. **Season** well with the salt and pepper.

At this point the soup is done and ready to serve, but wait—don't stop there. You serve it in bowls, buffet style, with a selection of the following toppings—your guests adding whatever they like. By the way, this is the ideal time to "clean out" the fridge:

> Crispy bacon pieces *if I said "bacon bits," you might buy those freaky artificial ones, and they would suck*

> Croutons or even crouton remnants from the bottom of the box

> Crispy, thin store-bought Asian noodles

> Shredded cheese *cheddar works nicely*

> Any hot sauce you like

> Diced leftover chicken, shrimp, turkey . . . *whatever*

> Anything else you can think of; *just look in the fridge*

Note: You put the whole deal out like a soup buffet and let everyone go for it. And, trust me, go for it they will. Don't forget the hot sauce and lots of good crusty bread.

Filipino Pork and Noodle Soup

Serves 4

You know how Jewish grandmothers are famous for their soup? The Filipino grandmothers are no different—except they use pork instead of chicken.

½ pound ground pork

½ large yellow onion, diced

2 cloves garlic, chopped fine

2 tablespoons olive oil

4 cups chicken broth

2 teaspoons freshly ground black pepper

¼ pound uncooked angel hair pasta

1 tablespoon soy sauce

2 large eggs, scrambled

½ cup finely chopped fresh cilantro

1 lime, cut into wedges

In a large pot, cook the pork with the onion and garlic in the oil over medium heat, stirring, until it's fully cooked, about 5 minutes. Add the broth and pepper and bring to a boil. Add the pasta and when it's ready, about 7 minutes, reduce the heat to a simmer. Add the soy sauce and scrambled eggs. Allow to thicken slightly and serve. The cilantro and lime wedges served on the side totally make it *so that means don't ignore them*.

French Onion Soup

Serves 6

Once again what you've been led to believe is tough to make—just isn't. Don't let the French convince you that this one is difficult, because if you can buy an onion, you can make this soup.

4 large yellow onions, thinly sliced *if you're not a knife whiz, take your time. It's all good, and there's no need to rush.*

2 teaspoons kosher salt

2 teaspoons freshly ground black pepper

3 tablespoons butter

¼ cup dry sherry

5 cups beef broth

3 cups 1-inch-cubed French bread *day-old if possible*

1½ cups grated Swiss cheese

2 tablespoons finely chopped fresh Italian parsley *the flat kind*

In a large pot, **season** the onions really well with the salt and pepper, then cook in the butter slowly over medium heat, stirring occasionally, until well browned. This will take 20 to 30 minutes. **Remove** from the heat *we don't want flames* and add the sherry. Put back on the heat and let it cook for a minute or two to burn off the alcohol—we only want the flavor. **Add** the beef broth, bring just to a boil over medium-high heat, then reduce the heat and simmer for 30 minutes. **Preheat** the broiler. **Ladle** the soup into ovenproof bowls, top with the bread cubes, then the cheese, and place under the broiler for a minute or two until it's all brown and bubbly. **Sprinkle** lightly with parsley before serving.

We named a show once "Things in Bowls."
Stupid name, great soups.

Blackened **Corn** Salad

What makes this so awesome are the little blackened bits of corn that happen during grilling. If you don't have the ears or the grill, you can make a pretty darn good version with canned corn—seriously. Like I'd lie about that?

4 ears corn, with husks and that *pain-in-the-ass*
silk removed, or one 15-ounce can whole
kernel corn, drained really well

3 tablespoons olive oil

1 red bell pepper, diced small

¼ cup finely chopped fresh cilantro

¼ cup red onion, diced small

½ to 1 teaspoon cayenne pepper

Juice from 1 lime

½ teaspoon kosher salt

4 ounces crumbled goat cheese

Preheat the grill to medium. **Brush** the corn with some of the olive oil and roast on the grill until softened, nicely browned, and charred in spots—this might take up to 30 minutes. Let cool. **Cut** the kernels off the cob and put in a bowl. (If using canned corn, heat one tablespoon of 1 oil in a nonstick skillet on high and cook the corn until really well cooked and black in spots—let cool. Put in a bowl.) **Add** all remaining ingredients, mix well, serve, and smile.

Green Bean and Tomato Salad

Serves 4

So fresh and so beautiful. Crispy, bright green beans served with beautiful, ripe red tomatoes. You better put this on a nice plate.

1 pound green beans

1 pound ripe tomatoes *not too squishy, but not too firm . . . just right*

3 tablespoons extra virgin olive oil

2 teaspoons balsamic vinegar

3 tablespoons shredded Parmesan cheese

Kosher salt and freshly ground black pepper to taste

Juice of half a lemon

Trim the ends from the green beans, cut into equal lengths, drop into a pot of boiling water, and cook until tender-crisp, about 3 minutes. When they're done, put the beans in ice water to **cool** and stop them cooking. **Trim** the tomato ends, cut into bite-size pieces, and put into a large bowl. **Drain** the beans and add to the tomatoes with the olive oil, vinegar, and 2 tablespoons of the Parmesan cheese. **Mix** well and season with salt and black pepper. To **serve**, put on serving plates, squeeze a little lemon over the top, and sprinkle with a little more Parmesan cheese and freshly ground black pepper.

Warm Cabbage Salad

Cool cabbage, topped with warm bacon, mush-rooms, and (store-bought) Dijon vinaigrette. Holy crap. You can even throw on some grilled chicken *(see A Perfectly Cooked Chicken Breast, page 107)* for a more substantial version. It's terrific. ***And how come people don't say "terrific" all that often anymore?***

6 cups thinly shredded napa cabbage

4 ounces blue cheese, crumbled

1 tablespoon olive oil

8 ounces sliced white mushrooms

One 2-ounce package "ready bacon," thinly sliced across the strips

6 ounces store-bought Dijon mustard vinaigrette

Freshly ground black pepper to taste

Put the shredded cabbage in a large bowl with the blue cheese on the top of it. **Preheat** a nonstick pan over medium heat and add the oil and mushrooms. **Cook**, stirring occasionally, until the 'shrooms are soft and starting to brown, 5 to 10 minutes. **Throw** in the bacon and cook, stirring occasionally, for another few minutes, until the bacon gets a bit crispy. **Add** the vinaigrette

Salad for Me?

Today was so beautiful out and I mean **really** beautiful. Of course you have no idea what day I'm talking about because I could have written this anytime. Anyway, it was one helluva day and all I could think of is that a salad would have tasted pretty darn good. But to really appreciate that comment, you need to know that I am *NOT* a salad guy. I almost never, and I mean *never*, think of having a salad. Oh sure, the occasional blue cheese wedge or warm cabbage number comes my way, but not without being followed by a perfectly rare steak. But it was so pretty, and so spring-like that a salad seemed just...right. Maybe you should have a salad—like right now?

to the mushroom-bacon mixture and bring to a quick simmer. **Pour** the heated dressing on the cabbage and cheese and toss really well. Put on serving plates and top with black pepper. **Serve** right away.

I finally realized a couple years ago that salads were not just for women's lunches. I was like, "Damn...this stuff is really good!" Go for it sometime; I think you'll be surprised.

Roasted Tomato and Goat Cheese Salad

Serves 6 *unless you eat all the tomatoes beforehand*

The magic is in the roasting of the tomatoes. They get all soft and amazing—and don't even get me started on what they do to crumbled goat cheese. It's almost sinful.

2 pounds small cherry tomatoes

2 fat cloves garlic, chopped fine

3 tablespoons extra-virgin olive oil

1 tablespoon balsamic vinegar

One 7-ounce bag mixed greens, your choice

8 ounces goat cheese, crumbled

Kosher salt and freshly ground black pepper to taste

Preheat the oven to 400°F. **Slice** the tomatoes in half, scoop out and discard the seeds, and put the tomato shells and garlic on a baking sheet. **Add** 1 tablespoon of the olive oil to the tomatoes and garlic and mix well. **Bake** until very tender and starting to brown, probably 25 to 30 minutes. When the tomatoes are almost finished cooking, **mix** the remaining 2 tablespoons of oil and the balsamic vinegar with the greens in a large bowl. **Distribute** the greens among the 6 plates and top each with the goat cheese. **Remove** the tomatoes from the oven, place some on each salad, and season with salt and pepper to taste. *Now the magic begins—the warm tomatoes start to melt the goat cheese and you suddenly have a much clearer idea of what heaven might be like...*

The Easiest Thing You Could Ever Do to a Fruit Salad

Serves 4

Simple and very pretty. This uses demerara sugar, or Sugar in the Raw—those little packets of heavily granulated brown sugar you see on tables at restaurants. You can buy the stuff in a one-pound box in the supermarket, or even in a box of a million little packets. But since you use so little in this recipe, it's easier just to "borrow" an extra one or two packs the next time you're at your local coffee shop. Look, I've spent so much money at those coffee joints that I figure they owe me at least a couple of small packets of the stuff.

3 cups mixed fresh fruit, a nice mix of melon and berries

¼ cup sour cream or crème fraîche
a very rich sour cream

2 packs Sugar in the Raw

Cut the fruit into bite-size pieces, but keep the berries whole.
To serve, **put** in pretty little glass bowls or martini glasses.
Top with a whack of sour cream or crème fraîche and
sprinkle lightly with the Sugar in the Raw.

Life happens at the last

Fast Food

minute sometimes—and your food can, too. The key here is make it good, make it easy, and make it—you guessed it—fast. I suppose another way to put it would be "Wham, bam, thank you, Sam"—but that would be, ah, just **stupid**. All of these dishes go from nothing to almost finished in about fifteen minutes, including cooking time. I know, I'm amazed myself.

Five-Minute Stir-Fry
Chip Bags Hot
O.F.R.B.P.J.G.O.
Sandwich Grilled
Grilled Lox and
Chipotle Mashed
Mashed Potatoes
Onion Mashed
and Potato Chip
Fried Egg Sandwich
Spinach and Garlic
Sandwich Sam's
Awww

Noodles Chili Corn Pastrami Wrap Grilled PB and Jelly Caprese Sandwich Fontina Sandwich Potatoes Horseradish Caramelized Red Potatoes Tomato Sandwich Double White Pizza with Late Night Turkey Kettle Corn Nuts!

Five-Minute
Stir-Fry Noodles

Serves 4

This is just one of those ridiculously easy little things that totally works. It makes the Styrofoam-packaged cup noodles almost restaurant-like. I also use these noodles in my Tomato Beef Chow Mein (page 182).

2 Styrofoam cups ramen-type instant noodles
the boiling water or microwave kind

1 tablespoon peanut oil

2 tablespoons teriyaki sauce

2 thinly sliced green onions (scallions), white and light green parts only, for garnish

Cook the noodles according to the package directions and drain well. **Heat** a wok or large skillet over very high heat, then add the oil. When the oil starts to smoke, throw in the noodles and quickly **stir-fry** about 30 seconds. **Add** the teriyaki sauce and **mix** well. To **serve**, remove to a plate and sprinkle with green onions. *Go on, call me a genius.*

Chili Corn Chip Bags

Makes 6 bags

This is one of those things that people make fun of until they try it. Then they're hooked. But you must have those little individual-sized bags of Fritos® for it—the fun is eating it right in the bag.

2 cups chili *any chili: yours, your mom's, or even chili out of a can—trust me, the can is easier*

6 Fritos® bags *the individual-sized ones*

½ cup shredded sharp cheddar cheese

Hot sauce to taste

This is going to seem stupid, but here goes: **Heat** the chili any way you want—*microwave, pot on the stove, or whatever works.* **Open** the Frito bag. **Spoon** chili into the bag—yes, **in** the bag. **Top** with some cheese, **in** the bag. **Add** some hot sauce, **in** the bag. **Add** a spoon and eat, **out** of the bag. *Stupid, but great.*

Hot Deli-Meat

There's this magical thing that happens when you heat up deli meat, and it's pretty amazing. Don't get me wrong—I like a cold turkey or roast beef sandwich as much as the next guy, but when the deli meat hits the heat, look out. Here are two of my favorites.

Hot Pastrami Wrap

Makes 6 wraps

Not only did this become an instant family classic in my house the night it was created, but it's also responsible for starting the hot deli-meat craze here.

One 8-ounce bag ready-mixed coleslaw *the store-bought bag kind with dressing included*
1 tablespoon adobo sauce *from a can of chipotle chiles*
1 pound deli-counter pastrami, thinly sliced
12 slices Muenster cheese
6 large flour tortillas or plain wraps

Make the coleslaw according to the package directions, stir in the adobo sauce, and set aside. **Separate** the pastrami slices into 6 little "piles" and cook both sides in a large nonstick skillet or griddle over medium heat. If you can't fit them all, don't—just do it in a couple of shifts. Cook for about 2 minutes per side. Once you've flipped each pile to brown it on the other side, place 2 pieces of cheese on top to melt. While the second side cooks, **warm** a tortilla or wrap slightly to soften, either in a nonstick skillet or in the microwave. **Place** a pastrami pile and some of the coleslaw on the wrap and roll up, burrito style (i.e., sides in, then roll up away from you). Give it a cool diagonal **cut** and start eating. You may never eat cold pastrami again.

O.F.R.B.P.J.G.O. (Open-Faced Roast Beef, Pepper Jack, and Grilled Onions)

Makes 5 open-faced sandwiches

You don't always need 2 slices of bread, do you? What...too little of a description?

1 tablespoon olive oil
1 large red onion, thinly sliced *okay, I'll admit it: I think I'm in love with red onions*
1 pound deli-counter roast beef, thinly sliced
3 onion kaiser rolls or suitable equivalent *no pressure here, but something like a hot dog bun just ain't gonna cut it*
5 slices pepper Jack cheese
¼ cup spicy brown mustard

Set a large nonstick skillet over medium heat and add the oil and the onion. **Cook**, stirring occasionally, until nicely browned and well softened, about 10 minutes. **Remove** from the pan, put in a bowl, and set aside. In the same skillet, **separate** the roast beef slices into 5 little "piles" and set over medium heat. While the "piles" are cooking, **stick** the sliced kaiser halves in the toaster until just slightly brown. When the roast beef has started to get a nice, golden-y brown color on the bottom, **flip** each little pile and add a slice of cheese on top. Allow the cheese to **melt** a bit. **Put** some mustard on each toasted kaiser half, and then **add** a bunch of the onions. **Remove** the roast beef from the skillet and put on top of the onion bed—and **eat**, of course.

I don't like to eat at fast-food places. It's not that I'm a food snob, it's that, well...ummm—ok, I guess I'm a food snob, *fine.*

Note: *These sands also make great appetizers. After grilling, just cut the sandwiches into triangles diagonally, lay out the diamonds all in a row on a cool-looking platter, and serve.*

Grilled PB and Jelly Sandwich

Makes 1 sandwich

This is not nearly as goofy as it seems. If you like a PB and J (and who doesn't?), then you'll love it when it's grilled. It gets all gooey when it cooks. It's brilliant.

Not only are grilled sammies quick, but they're amazingly versatile: a lunch (obviously), a simple dinner, a late-night snack, a breakfast (in college), and possibly the best hangover cure known to man—there's just something about food that's buttered and then grilled.

Peanut butter, *try creamy*
Jelly, *try raspberry*
2 slices bread, *try whole wheat*
Butter, softened

Spread the PB and J between bread slices and close. **Butter** one side of the bread and place, butter side down, in a heated nonstick skillet. **Squish** down a little with a spatula while it cooks. **Grill** until the bottom is nicely browned, then butter the top, flip and repeat. Trust me, you'll like it.

Grilled Caprese Sandwich

Makes 1 sandwich

2 slices sourdough bread
1 ripe, medium-sized tomato, thinly sliced and enough to cover a slice of the bread
Fresh basil leaves (enough to completely cover a slice of the bread)

Grilled Sandwiches

You know that simple little fresh mozzarella, basil, and tomato salad we all love to eat? This is like that—but only in a sandwich.

Fresh mozzarella cheese *the kind that comes packed in water,* **thinly sliced and enough to completely cover a slice of the bread**
Butter, softened

Build it like this: bread, tomato slices, basil leaves, cheese, bread. **Butter** one side of the bread and place, butter side down, in a heated nonstick skillet. **Squish** down a little with a spatula while it cooks. **Grill** until the bottom is nicely browned, then butter the top, flip and repeat.

Grilled Lox and Fontina Sandwich

Makes 1 sandwich

Lox (salmon that's been cured) is the unofficial food of my people and it completely rules. Doesn't sound good, you think? Are we judging a food by its name...?

Fontina cheese, thinly sliced and enough to cover the bread twice
2 slices bread *I lean toward a heavy white here*
Lox, thinly sliced and enough to double-cover a slice of bread
Butter for grilling

Place a layer of the cheese on 1 slice of the bread. **Cover** with all the lox. **Place** the second layer of cheese on the lox and top with the second slice of bread. **Butter** one side of the bread and place, butter side down, in a heated nonstick skillet. **Squish** down a little with a spatula or carefully with your hand while it cooks. **Grill** until the bottom is nicely browned, then butter the top, **flip**, and repeat.

Mashed Potatoes

Let me say this up front—it's okay to use frozen, packaged, or even dried mashed potatoes. They're all really made from potatoes, plus by the time you add a bunch of extra stuff to them, even your grandmother couldn't tell they weren't from scratch. This is just a guide, but you can add almost anything to them you want—goat cheese, sour cream, bits of roast beef, rice pudding, quickly sautéed vegetables, crunchy rice noodles. By the way, I was just kidding about the rice pudding. I hate rice pudding. In fact I don't even like the name and I **LOVE** rice.

Chipotle Mashed Potatoes

Makes 2 cups

These would be great with the Mahi Mahi with Salsa Cream on page 174.

2 cups hot cooked mashed potatoes
1 tablespoon adobo sauce (from a can of chipotle chiles)
1 tablespoon finely chopped fresh cilantro
3 tablespoons shredded Monterey Jack cheese

Mix together the potatoes, adobo sauce, and cilantro. While the potatoes are still hot, **garnish** with the cheese and watch it melt. **Serve**.

Three Easy Ways

Horseradish Mashed Potatoes

Makes 2 cups

Not only are they good, but they're fun to say.

2 cups hot cooked mashed potatoes
1 fat tablespoon prepared horseradish
1 tablespoon finely chopped fresh Italian parsley
the flat kind
Kosher salt and freshly ground black pepper to taste

Mix together the potatoes, horseradish, and parsley. **Season** with salt and pepper and **serve**.

Caramelized Red Onion Mashed Potatoes

Makes 2 cups

These are my fave.

1 red onion *of course*, **very thinly sliced**
2 to 3 tablespoons good extra virgin olive oil
1 tablespoon brown sugar
2 cups hot cooked mashed potatoes

Cook the red onion in about a tablespoon of the oil in a nonstick skillet over medium heat, stirring occasionally, until very soft and beginning to brown, about 10 minutes. **Add** the brown sugar and stir well. **Serve** the mashed potatoes with a big whack of the onions on top and a good drizzle of the olive oil. *I want to swear here because they're so good, but I won't.*

I always have the makings of both of these in the house—and so should you.

Tomato and Potato Chip Sandwich

Makes 1 sandwich

I've eaten this about once a month since I was eighteen. So that makes for a total of about . . . umm . . . ahh . . . never mind. It's pretty much the perfect late-night food.

1 tablespoon tangy mayonnaise, like Heinz Salad Cream
2 slices white bread (trust me with the white here)
½ medium-sized ripe tomato, thinly sliced
Freshly ground black pepper to taste
1 BIG handful plain potato chips

Spread the mayo on one of the bread slices. **Top** with the tomato slices. Season well with the pepper—don't be shy. **Place** a **BIG** handful of chips on each and gently **balance** the second slice of bread on top of the chips. Now **squish** the whole thing down with your hand, cut in half, and eat. *Seriously, there are no words . . .*

My Dogs Eat Dog Food

I know some will find this an odd concept, but we don't feed our pets people food, and neither should you. With all the food being cooked around my house people are always amazed that Haley & Lucky don't beg, and they don't because they know they won't get anything. We shouldn't eat their stuff, and they shouldn't eat our stuff—it's that simple.

Double Fried Egg Sandwich

Makes 1 sandwich

It's seems crazy having a simple fried egg sandwich recipe in a book, but I'm always amazed how many people have never had one—so here goes.

1 teaspoon butter
2 large eggs
2 slices whole wheat bread
1 slice cheese, whatever you've got but I dig
  provolone here
1 tablespoon mayonnaise

Heat a nonstick pan over medium heat, **melt** the butter, and **fry** the eggs, breaking the yolks. While the eggs cook, **toast** the bread. When you flip the eggs over, **add** the cheese to the top of one of them. **Spread** the mayo on the toast, place the fried eggs on the toast on top of one another, and top with the other slice of toast. *If this is your first fried egg sandwich, I'll bet it won't be your last.*

Note: About the only thing you could add to this would be a splash of hot sauce. I don't do it, but you might like it. Oh, and maybe some bacon.

White Pizza with Spinach and Garlic

Makes one 12-inch pizza

No red tomato sauce-y pizza—change is good, you know? And if you kept a pizza crust in the freezer like I told you to at the beginning of this book, you'd be about 14 minutes from eating right now. But nooooooooo, you had to do it your own way, didn't you? Well, what are you going to eat now, hotshot?

One 12-inch ready-made pizza crust
½ tablespoon olive oil
3 cloves garlic, roughly chopped
One 10-ounce bag fresh spinach leaves
3 ounces feta cheese, crumbled
4 to 6 slices provolone cheese
½ cup shredded mozzarella cheese

Preheat the oven to 425°F. Lightly **rub** or brush the crust with the olive oil. **Heat** a skillet over medium heat, add the oil, then add the garlic and cook, stirring, for about 30 seconds. **Add** the spinach and stir until wilted. This won't take more than about a minute. **Sprinkle** the feta over the crust. **Spread** the spinach and garlic over the feta and then add the slices of provolone. **Top** with the shredded mozzarella. **Bake** for 12 to 15 minutes, or until the crust starts to brown and the cheese gets all melty, then serve in wedges.

Late Night Grilled Turkey Sandwich

Makes 5 sandwiches

Okay, so technically you're not really "making" anything with this recipe—you're just "putting it together". . . but is that so bad? I don't think so, because this is so good. Plus, I often find myself making this at about 1:00 a.m.—and at that time I just wanna eat, I don't wanna work.

1 pound deli-counter turkey, thinly sliced

5 bagels, pick any kind you like

3 tablespoons mayonnaise

2 tablespoons spicy brown mustard

2 tablespoons honey

5 big slices Muenster, provolone, or any cheese you like, thinly sliced

1 large tomato, cut into 5 slices

Heat a large nonstick pan over medium heat. **Separate** the turkey slices into 5 "piles" and put them in the pan (with no butter, oil, no nothing). While the meat is cooking, **slice** the bagels in half and **toast** them. **Mix** the mayo with the mustard and honey. When the turkey starts to brown, **flip** it and place a slice of the cheese on top of each pile. Allow the cheese to **melt**, then remove the pan from the heat. **Spread** the honeyed mayo mix on one half of each bagel, add a pile of "cooked" turkey and a tomato slice, then top each with the other bagel side and slice in half.

Sam's Kettle Corn

Makes about 4 cups

Sure, you could get this if you worked at the fair, but isn't it nice to know you can make it yourself without having to live in a trailer married to the bearded lady?

I appreciate the fact that if you're making food for a sporting event, you might not want to also make your own snacks. But I'm here to tell you, you can. Your guests will be all, "You made what? Come on . . . you can't make this stuff? And now you're going to tell us you also made those amazing Sam's Sticky Sweet BBQ Ribs (page 130)." You just smile, walk in the kitchen, and reward yourself with another Sammy-Boy's Margarita (page 126).

½ cup popcorn
¼ cup vegetable oil
¼ cup sugar
Kosher salt to taste

Put the popcorn, oil, and sugar in a large pot. **Stir** so all of the kernels are covered with the sugar/oil mixture. **Turn** the heat to medium, cover the pot with the lid, and wait. Once popping begins, **shake** the pot continuously to keep the kernels from sticking to the bottom and burning. When the popping slows, **remove** from the heat and pour into a bowl. When slightly cool, **separate** the big clumps, **season** lightly with the kosherness, and **eat**.

Quick Snacks

Awww Nuts!

Makes 2 cups

Sweet and spicy at the same time, these little guys are hard to put down. Feel free to adjust the spices to your own taste. But, hey, I've just gotten a bunch of Emmys. Why should you listen to me?

2 tablespoons oil *peanut or vegetable is fine—olive is not*
1 cup lightly salted peanuts, shelled
1 cup lightly salted cashews
1 tablespoon chili powder
½ teaspoon cayenne pepper
1 tablespoon sugar

Preheat the oil in a large nonstick skillet over medium heat. When the oil is hot, **add** the nuts, chili powder, and cayenne and **mix** thoroughly. **Remove** from the heat and stir in the sugar well. Bingo! That's it. Let cool slightly, pour into a bowl, and **serve**.

A lot of thinking goes into

Just Chicken

figuring out what to say at the beginning of each chapter in a cookbook...or it's supposed to. Three or four sentences, my editor Justin said, would be fine. But this chapter is about chicken. Please, what the **heck** do you say about chicken? "It's beige and can go in a lot of things?" I mean, it's just chicken after all.

But before you charge ahead, maybe you need to go read my words on one of the greatest inventions of the past couple hundred years: the "deli-roasted chicken." It's in Basic Stuff to Know, page 5.

A Perfectly Cooked

Chicken Enchiladas

Chicken Quesadilla

Chicken Breasts

Cheese and Sun-

BBQ Chicken Pizza

Sandwich Halloween

Chicken Breast
Hot-Sweet Wings
Adobo Chicken
Stuffed with Goat
Dried Tomato Pesto
Rosemary Chicken
Chicken Chili

A Perfectly Cooked Chicken Breast

Makes 1 chicken breast

Chicken breasts are notoriously difficult to cook. That's a nice way of saying they're a pain in the ass. Thick on one end and thin on the other, you just can't win—so don't even bother. The key is to level the "chicken playing field," so to speak.

1 boneless, skinless chicken breast

½ tablespoon olive oil

Kosher salt and freshly ground black pepper

Place the chicken breast in a large resealable plastic bag and close the bag. Using something heavy *I favor a full bottle of vodka*, **pound** the breast to an even thickness of about ½ inch. **Remove** from the bag, drizzle with the olive oil, and season with the salt and pepper on both sides. Now you can **grill** it, **panfry** it, or **whatever**—and when you do, the breast will cook evenly. You're probably looking at no more than 3 to 4 minutes a side, whatever cooking method you use. *Just don't burn the hell out of it.* You want it juicy and tender.

And if you need an idea for what to do with it, try:

> **Grilled Chicken Caesar:** Use a ready-to-go bag of Caesar salad from the vegetable aisle at the supermarket, mixed with a little more grated Parmesan cheese, some fresh ground black pepper, and a squeeze of lemon juice, and top it with A Perfectly Cooked Chicken Breast, sliced thin.

> **Pasta with Chicken:** Almost any pasta dish will benefit from the addition of some nicely cooked or grilled chicken.

> **Simple Grilled Chicken Tacos:** This one's grilled, sliced thin, and thrown in a warmed tortilla with the Super Simple Mango Salsa from page 157.

> **Panfried Chicken & Mushrooms:** This is a nice mix of a few different varieties of mushrooms, sliced and cooked in some olive oil until really soft, served on top of the chicken with not much more than fresh ground black pepper and a good drizzle of extra virgin olive oil.

Ever wonder why chicken is so darned expensive to buy in the supermarket? I don't, but every time I see footage of a chicken farm there's about a jillion of them running around. You'd think that would make them cheap—guess not.

Chicken **Enchiladas**

Serves 8

This thing comes out of the oven all bubbly and beautiful, with the cream and cheese having magically made their own amazing sauce. Trust me, you're going to want to eat these all yourself—but don't. That would be a big mistake.

3 cups shredded cooked chicken (from a pre-cooked deli-roasted chicken)

1 cup store-bought salsa verde (green salsa)

One 4-ounce can diced green chiles

2 tablespoons finely chopped canned chipotle chiles

2 cups whipping cream

1 cup chicken broth

8 flour tortillas, fajita size (about 8 inches in diameter)

1½ cups shredded Monterey Jack cheese

Fresh cilantro, chopped fine for garnish

Preheat the oven to 350°F. In a bowl, **mix** the chicken, salsa, green chiles, and chipotles together well. **Pour** half of the cream into the bottom of a 9 × 13–inch baking dish. **Pour** the chicken broth into a wide bowl and submerge a flour tortilla until well moistened, about 30 seconds. **Remove** and place about ⅛ of the chicken mixture in the middle of the tortilla, roll it up like a cigar, and place it, seam side down, on the cream in the baking dish. **Repeat** until all the tortillas are filled and side by side in the dish. **Spread** the cheese over the enchiladas and pour the remaining 1 cup cream over the top. **Bake** until starting to brown nicely, about 30 minutes, and serve with a little cilantro.

Note: Sometimes we, *I mean I*, will make 2 pans, cook them both, and then eat one pan and freeze one for another day.

Pretend Something Doesn't Exist Anymore

There's a game I occasionally like to play when I go grocery shopping—and no, it's not the one where I put random things in people's carts when they're not looking. That's a great one, but not the one I'm talking about. I pretend that one of the items I need for a recipe no longer exists and I'm forced to substitute it with something else. Let's say every Tuesday for the past three years you've made your Aunt Ruth's Chicken—chicken, apricot jam, bread crumbs... something like that—you get the idea. Just find a sub for any ingredient. Of course turkey for the chicken or peach jam for the apricot would be a no-brainer, but what about crushed-up Cap'n Crunch® cereal instead of the bread crumbs? Now you're thinking. The idea is to try something new instead of the everyday.

Hot-Sweet Wings

Makes about 20 wings

Make 'em at a moment's notice by keeping a bag of store-bought wings (see Note) in the freezer. The best part is you don't even need to defrost them first—just yank 'em out and throw 'em in the oven. It's a piece of cake . . . I mean, piece of chicken.

3 pounds chicken wings

½ cup honey

4 tablespoons (½ stick) butter

6 ounces Louisiana-style hot sauce *like "Frank's"*

½ to 1 teaspoon cayenne pepper

Preheat the broiler. **Cover** a large baking sheet with aluminum foil *to make cleanup easier* and spread out the wings. **Broil** until the tops of the wings are nicely browned and cooked, 10 to 15 minutes. *If there is a lot of liquid, you may need to drain the baking sheet at this point.* **Flip** the wings, return to the broiler, and broil until nicely browned on the other side, at least 10 minutes more. While the second side cooks, **combine** the honey, butter, hot sauce, and cayenne in a small pot and simmer over medium-low heat. When the wings are done, **toss**

Cook with Your Grandparents

I remember talking with friends

one day about how my grandparents had passed away before I was old enough to really appreciate them. I said it would be cool to be able to "cook with my grandmas" if just for one meal. There's something about cooking with someone that sort of breaks down barriers. For example, if I put my kids in a room with their two grandmothers, the conversation would be a bit sterile. "How is school, how are your friends...," etc. But in a cooking situation, the natural conversation is about the food but can very comfortably transition to other things, like this:

Grandmother: "So it's important to dice the chicken into small pieces. You know, this reminds me of the time your grandfather took a bet and ran naked through the chicken coop of old man McGeary's farm. Boy, was he something in those days..."

If you have kids, get them to cook with your parents. And if you're a kid, go find a grandparent and cook with them. And if you don't have any grandparents, just go borrow one or two. You'll all be better off for it.

them in batches into the pot to coat them with the sauce. **Remove** to a platter. **Serve** with the extra sauce on the side.

Note: I say "wings," but they're often sold with wings and small leg kinda things. It's all good. Don't get too hung up on the terminology.

Chicken **Quesadilla**

Serves 2

This was the first recipe I ever made on TV—wow, I haven't thought about it in a while. Hang on while I have a "moment" to myself. Okay, I'm good now. It's an appetizer, a dinner when you toss a salad with it, or even a late snack after a night of cocktails. Here's that deli-roasted chicken again . . .

1 cup shredded cooked chicken (from a precooked deli chicken)

¼ cup shredded mixed Monterey Jack and cheddar cheese

3 green onions (scallions), white and light green parts only, diced fine

½ teaspoon ground cumin

2 flour tortillas, about 8 inches in diameter

For garnish

Sour cream

Your favorite salsa

Fresh cilantro, chopped fine

Preheat a large nonstick skillet over medium heat. **Mix** the chicken, cheese, green onions, and cumin together in a bowl. **Place** one of the tortillas in the skillet, cover it with the chicken mixture, and place the second tortilla on top. **Press** down with a spatula to flatten. Once the bottom starts to brown, after about 3 minutes, **flip** it over and brown the other side. **Remove** the quesadilla, cut into wedges, and serve with the sour cream, salsa, and cilantro.

Note: Try this on your BBQ sometime. All the steps are the same—just swap your grill for your skillet.

Make this a goal in your life:

NOT to ever dry out chicken again.

Adobo Chicken

Simple chicken cooked in soy sauce with garlic is the unofficial dish of the Philippines. But this . . . in a bowl . . . on a bed of steamed rice . . . is like . . . totally . . . wow. Poetic, huh?

1 cup soy sauce

½ cup white vinegar

5 cloves garlic, chopped fine

2 tablespoons brown sugar

1 tablespoon freshly ground black pepper

3 bay leaves

3 pounds chicken thighs, bone in

Combine the soy sauce, vinegar, garlic, sugar, pepper, and bay leaves in the bottom of a large pot. **Place** the chicken, skin side down, in the pot and bring to a boil. Immediately turn the heat down to a **simmer** and cover with the lid. After 30 minutes, **remove** the lid, turn the chicken over, **simmer** for an additional 20 to 30 minutes, then **serve**. If you've read my thoughts on rice cookers in Basic Stuff to Know on page 13, you know how easy it will be to serve this on freshly steamed white rice.

Chicken Breasts Stuffed with Goat Cheese and Sun-Dried Tomato Pesto

Serves 4

It's really only three main ingredients, but it sounds pretty fancy, right? Most good supermarkets sell sun-dried tomato pesto. And now that you know how easy it is to stuff chicken breasts, go wild and use anything you like: mushrooms, nuts, fruit, or even stuffing itself.

4 boneless, skinless chicken breasts *big ones*

4 ounces goat cheese *the soft log kind is easier for this, instead of the crumbled*

¼ cup jarred sun-dried tomato pesto

Wooden skewers, soaked in water for about 30 minutes

Olive oil

Kosher salt and freshly ground black pepper

Preheat a grill to medium-high (or preheat the broiler).

Put the chicken breasts in a resealable plastic bag and hit them gently with something heavy, like a bottle, to flatten them a bit—not a lot, just enough to make them slightly wider and a little more even, thickness-wise. Make a wide, deep slice in the side of each breast to form a pocket. Stuff each pocket with both some of the cheese and pesto. Use a couple of wooden skewers to seal the opening shut. Drizzle with olive oil and season well with salt and pepper on both sides. Grill (or broil) on both sides until done, about 10 minutes per side, and serve right away, because when they're hot, they'll get all drippy when you cut into them.

Don't Feel Like You Have to Cook Everything for a Gathering

Just because you've decided to have people over doesn't mean you have to make every last little thing yourself. Here are some tips:

> Make a few things and buy a few things. Will anyone care that the potato salad came from the store? Only if it blows, so buy a decent one. And make it look good—a nice bowl and a little garnish won't kill you.

> Ask a couple of the guests to bring something. People are generally so thrilled they don't have to have the party at their place they're only too happy to bring food. But tell them exactly what you want—if you leave it up to them they might bring the same potato salad you just bought.

BBQ Chicken
Pizza

BBQ sauce, chicken, and cheese were just made for one another. Another deli-roasted chicken miracle. One chicken will make 2 of these pizzas.

2½ cups shredded cooked chicken
  (from a precooked deli-roasted chicken)
½ cup favorite BBQ sauce
One ready-made pizza crust, like a Boboli
½ small red onion, thinly sliced
½ cup shredded mozzarella cheese
3 tablespoons finely chopped fresh cilantro

Preheat the oven to 425°F. In a bowl, **mix** the cooked chicken with about 3 tablespoons of the BBQ sauce. **Brush** the remaining sauce over the pizza crust. **Spread** the chicken over the crust, cover with the onion, and top with the mozzarella. **Bake** until the top starts to brown and get bubbly, 10 to 12 minutes. **Remove** from the oven, sprinkle with the cilantro, cut into wedges, and serve.

Note: *In a pinch,* read: "emergency," *when I couldn't get my hands on a deli-roasted chicken, I've bought the pregrilled kind of chicken strips—sold in resealable zipper-top bags in the cheese-butter aisle at the supermarket—and they've worked just fine.*

Rosemary Chicken Sandwich

Serves 4

This is a staple in the Cooking Guy house. You can change the flavor of this simple sandwich just by changing a couple of the ingredients. For an Asian-style san', you might try using a teriyaki marinade and leaving out the rosemary and dressing. Or for a Mediterranean version, you'd just swap the avocado for feta cheese— I think you're getting the idea.

4 boneless, skinless chicken breasts, flattened (see Note)

12 ounces favorite Italian dressing

3 tablespoons chopped fresh rosemary leaves

1 loaf ciabatta (bread), available at many supermarkets

1 tablespoon olive oil

2 ripe avocados, pitted and sliced medium thin

2 ripe tomatoes, sliced medium thin

Freshly ground black pepper

Place the flattened chicken breasts in a large casserole pan. In a bowl, combine the dressing and rosemary well and pour over the chicken, making sure the pieces are fully covered.

Allow to marinate at least 15 minutes to an hour. **Preheat** a grill to medium-high. **Grill** the chicken on both sides until it's done the way you like, 4 to 5 minutes per side—and for God's sake, try not to overcook it. *Or if the weather totally stinks, you could always heat up the broiler and throw the chicken under for about 5 minutes a side.* **Slice** the ciabatta down the middle lengthwise and then into 4 sandwich-size sections, brush each side with olive oil, and **grill** until you've got those cool grill marks on each side. **Assemble** the sandwich: bread, chicken, avocado, tomato, pepper, bread.

Note: *To flatten a chicken breast, place it in a large resealable plastic bag and close the bag. Using something heavy I favor a full bottle of vodka, pound the breast to an even thickness of about ½ inch.*

Go Cruise the Aisles of an Ethnic Supermarket

What better way to learn about O.P.F. (other people's food) than by going to where they shop? Head out on a Saturday morning and explore: Japanese, Chinese, Indian, Russian—it's all good. And trust me, everyone loves sharing their world with newcomers. They'll be overjoyed to answer all your questions.

Halloween Chicken Chili

Serves 8

Over the years this has become such a Halloween trick-or-treating tradition in our house that our neighbor Doug always shows up at our front door like one of Pavlov's dogs with his own bowl, looking for his annual share. You've gotta love stuff like that.

4 cans Great Northern white beans *they're already softened and require no soaking*

1 small yellow onion, diced small

4 cloves garlic, chopped fine

1 tablespoon olive oil

2 cups chicken broth

2 cups shredded cooked chicken (from a precooked deli chicken)

One 4-ounce can diced green chiles

2 teaspoons ground cumin

2 teaspoons cayenne pepper

2 teaspoons dried oregano

1 French or sourdough baguette, cut into 2-inch pieces

Fresh Italian parsley *the flat kind*, **chopped fine for garnish**

Drain the beans. In a medium pot, **cook** the onion and garlic in the oil over medium heat, stirring, until softened. **Add** the broth, chicken, chiles, spices and you're done. Okay, so you actually need to let the whole thing **simmer** 10 to 15 minutes to let it all heat through. To **serve**, place a couple pieces of bread in a bowl and top with the chili. Sprinkle with a little fresh chopped parsley. *Wait 15 minutes, and Doug will be over.*

What a ridiculous name for

My
Favorites

a chapter. Exactly how is this supposed to be helpful to you at all? I mean, just because *I* love something doesn't mean *you* will, right? Maybe, maybe not. But it's my book, and I can do what I like (make that whatever my editor will let me get away with . . .)

So I'll tell you what makes something one of my favorites. If we like it and cook it a lot at home, for family or friends, it's a favorite. If we hate it and never cook it, then it's not even in this book. For example, the Black Bean Salmon we make all the time is a favorite and therefore in this chapter. The peanut butter pizza I tried to make a couple weeks ago is not.

Sammy-Boy's Bean Salmon Sam's Sticky Fridge Fried Rice Mixed Jambalaya Pizza Steak Salad Crumbles Day-Omelet Mac and with Bacon My Lemon Pasta

Margarita Black
Shrimp Tacos
Sweet BBQ Ribs
Rice Cooker
Buffalo Chicken
with Blue Cheese
After Stuffing
(Blue) Cheese
Mom's Lox Dip
with Mint

Sammy-Boy's Margarita

Makes 1 *(go on, be selfish)*

I say one good cocktail is way better than two lousy ones—and this is a perfect example of that. But I have this theory: crappy tequila makes a crappy Margarita. So use something decent. And be careful . . . these are strong.

Ice

2 ounces good tequila

1 ounce sweet-and-sour mix
   DO NOT *substitute with Margarita mix*

½ ounce Grand Marnier

1 lime

1 orange

1 splash Rose's lime juice

Fill a cocktail shaker a third of the way with ice and add the tequila, sweet-and-sour mix, Grand Marnier, the juice from ½ lime, juice from ¼ orange, and a splash of the Rose's lime juice. **Place** on the lid and shake like a fool—you want it icy. **Add** fresh ice to a glass and pour in the Margarita from the shaker. **Squeeze** a wedge each of the lime and orange on top and drop the wedges into the glass. **Float** a little more Grand Marnier over the top and, voilà! Life is good.

Note: If you want to do something cool, grate some lime zest on top of a dish of kosher salt. Then dip the rim of your glass in some Grand Marnier and push it into the lime-zested salt.

Black Bean Salmon

I put this near the top because we serve it a ton when people come over. It's simple, delicious, and has only three main ingredients, but it tastes like it has fifty. You can find the garlic and black bean sauce in the Asian aisle of almost any supermarket. What helps make this great is that the salmon is broiled instead of baked—which means not only does it look amazing, but it's not all dried out.

1 cup apricot preserves *which is pretty much the same as jam, isn't it?*

⅓ cup "black bean and garlic sauce"

1 whole salmon fillet, about 2 pounds

2 tablespoons finely chopped green onions (scallions), white and light green parts only

Sesame seeds

Preheat the broiler to high. In a small bowl, **combine** the apricot jam and black bean sauce and mix well. **Cover** a baking sheet with foil *for easy cleanup later* and spray with nonstick stuff. **Lay** the salmon on the foil. **Spoon** the sauce over the top to cover all of the salmon. **Broil** for about 7 minutes for about every inch of salmon thickness *not inch of salmon length, because that would be really bad*. **Remove** to a platter, sprinkle with the green onions and sesame seeds, and serve. **Prepare** to be congratulated.

Shrimp Tacos

Makes 6 tacos

I say it all the time: keep a bag of raw, shell-on shrimp in the freezer for easy last-minute recipes like this one. The chipotle–sour cream–lime mix that goes with this is so good. But don't get all freaked out with chipotles—you just buy them in a little can in the supermarket in the Spanish-products aisle. Actually, you should buy two cans— I also use them in my Chicken Enchiladas (page 108) and my Chunky Guacamole (page 57).

½ cup sour cream

1 chipotle from the can, chopped fine (see Note)

2 limes

1 tablespoon peanut oil

½ pound raw shrimp, peeled and cut into smallish pieces

½ tablespoon Old Bay seasoning

6 corn tortillas (about 5 inches in diameter), warmed well (either in a nonstick pan or even in the microwave)

½ cup shredded purple cabbage

In a small bowl, **mix** together the sour cream, chipotle, and juice from half a lime. Set aside. **Preheat** a skillet really well over high heat and then add the oil.

I use my carbon steel flat-bottomed wok for this, by the way. **Add** the shrimp and stir-fry quickly—they will cook fast. You're looking for them to essentially go white. When they get there, **hit** them with the Old Bay and juice from the other half a lime. **Give** 'em a quick couple of stirs, and you're done.

I like to put everything out and let people make their own. Put some of the chipotle cream on a tortilla, add a little cabbage, add the shrimp, and squeeze a little more fresh lime juice over the top. If it wasn't obvious, this goes amazingly well with my Margarita recipe on page 126.

Note: Use only "1" chipotle and not "1 can." If you use a whole can, like my father-in-law once did, you'll talk like "thith" for a week.

Force Yourself to Have at Least One Good Party a Year

What better way to practice what you've learned? But I'm not referring to the "pizza & keg" type of days gone by. I mean a proper, we're-adults-now kinda party. A little work, a little planning, but a lot of fun. And when you've got one under your belt, the next one will be a breeze.

Sam's Sticky Sweet BBQ Ribs

Serves 4

Every so often a recipe gains almost "celebrity-like" status, and this is one of them. Store-bought BBQ sauce with only brown sugar and pancake syrup makes these ribs glisten with sticky, finger-lickin' sweetness. The vinegar helps make them falling-off-the-bone tender. So let's recap: they're sticky, sweet, messy, and falling-off tender. Better get the napkins ready.

2 racks pork back ribs, 4 to 5 pounds total

4 tablespoons white vinegar

1½ cups plain BBQ sauce

¼ cup pancake syrup

¼ cup brown sugar

Preheat the oven to 400°F. **Place** the ribs and vinegar in a large baking (casserole) dish and cover tightly with aluminum foil. **Bake** until the ribs are very fork-tender between the bones, about 90 minutes. In a small bowl, **mix** together the BBQ sauce, syrup, and brown sugar and set aside. **Remove** the ribs from the oven and carefully lift off the foil—there will be a ton of steam. The ribs are now fully cooked and just need to be "sauced" and "colored" on the grill. **Preheat** a grill to medium and place

the ribs, meat side down—they don't need sauce yet. **Cook** until they start to develop grill marks. **Turn** over and now baste the top. You could stop here after they grill a bit on this side, or you could baste them a bit more and then give them a couple more minutes with the meat side down—*that's what I do*. Give 'em one extra **baste** after they've been removed, put on your crown, your Highness, and serve.

Note: No BBQ grill? No problem. Heat your broiler and put them under for maybe up to 5 minutes a side. You're looking for good color; even slightly black spots are cool. But jet black and smoking . . . no.

Fridge Fried Rice

Makes 6 to 8 servings

I was going to call this "whatever the hell you've got in the fridge fried rice," but that seemed a little long. The key is having a little leftover rice—which, if you use a rice cooker like me, is no problem because it's easy to have extra. You just want to open the fridge and go for it—leftover chicken, steak, vegetables—it's all good. Whatever you've got, just cut it up and throw it in.

1 tablespoon peanut oil

1 cup of the following "whatever"—carrots (or any vegetable), green onions (scallions) (white and light green parts only), cooked steak, cooked chicken, cooked turkey, or even cooked the-other-white-meat—all sliced into thin pieces

One 2-ounce pack "ready bacon," thinly sliced

4 to 6 cups cooked rice, cold

2 large eggs, beaten

3 tablespoons soy sauce

1 teaspoon sesame oil

2 tablespoons green onions (scallions), white and light green parts only, thinly sliced for garnish

Preheat a large nonstick pan or wok over medium-high heat with the peanut oil. If using uncooked vegetables, **add** them to the wok and stir-fry for a couple of minutes until everything softens but is still a bit crisp. If not, skip to the next step. Now **add** anything already cooked (except the rice)—the bacon, the meat, the whatever—and cook for a couple of minutes. *We're heating here.* **Add** the rice and stir well to break up and heat through. In a small bowl, **beat** the eggs, **stir** in the soy sauce and sesame oil, then add to the wok or pan. **Stir** the whole mess until the eggs are mixed in well and cooked through. **Serve** topped with the green onions.

Don't Expect What You Can't Get

It's a simple concept that keeps me from being disappointed when I go out to eat. I won't go to a restaurant that specializes in, say, oatmeal and expect the foie gras to be top drawer, because it probably won't. I wouldn't go to Bucky's House of Head Cheese and expect them to offer a "seared diver scallop with a hint of truffle" because it's not what they do. (Now that I think of it, head cheese is nothing that *anyone* should do.) The key is to know what a place does and appreciate it for that. You'll be a lot happier. I know you can argue that if something is on the menu they should be able to make it well, but sometimes they can't and shouldn't. Just because I can run, it doesn't mean I should be in the 400 in the Olympics, right?

Rice Cooker Mixed Jambalaya

Serves 8 to 10

The beauty here is that everything goes into the rice cooker. You turn it on and split. It's as simple as pie, or in this case as simple as jambalaya—which normally tends to be not so simple.

1 pound spicy smoked sausage (fully cooked), cut lengthwise and then into ¼-inch half circles

1 pound large raw shrimp, peeled and deveined
31/40s are ideal

8 ounces (about 2 cups) shredded cooked chicken (from a deli-roasted chicken)

1½ cups uncooked white rice

4 cups chicken broth

One 4-ounce can diced green chiles

2 tablespoons Creole seasoning (sold in the supermarket spice aisle)

Chopped cilantro, for garnish

Put all ingredients except for the cilantro into a rice cooker, **mix** well, and turn on. When the rice cooker goes off, it's ready. **Garnish** with cilantro.

Buffalo Chicken Pizza

Makes one 12-inch pizza

Confused? Don't be. This is all the great taste of those spicy little chicken wings, except in a pizza—and no bones to deal with.

4 tablespoons (½ stick) butter

4 tablespoons hot sauce—not like Tabasco but more a Louisiana-style *"Frank's" is good*

2½ cups shredded cooked chicken (from a precooked deli chicken)

½ cup blue cheese salad dressing
any kind, but the chunkier, the better

One 12-inch ready-made pizza crust, like Boboli

1 cup shredded mozzarella

2 tablespoons finely chopped fresh cilantro

Preheat the oven to 425°F. In a small pot, melt the butter with the hot sauce, stir well, and remove from the heat. **Add** the chicken and mix well. **Spread** the blue cheese dressing on the pizza crust, then top with the chicken mixture. (Don't worry if it's messy, because it will be.) **Top** with the mozzarella. **Bake** until bubbly, brown, and awesome looking, 12 to 15 minutes. **Sprinkle** with the cilantro, cut into wedges, and serve.

Steak Salad with Blue Cheese Crumbles

Serves 4

There's nothing particularly earth shattering about a steak salad—other than that it's really, really great. We all just don't make it often enough. And though the standard is a cold steak salad, I like it with a just-off-the-grill steak still warm, because it makes the blue cheese all soft and wonderful.

2 steaks, each about ¾ pound *New Yorks would make an excellent choice*

Kosher salt and freshly ground black pepper

1 bag prewashed mixed greens

4 ripe tomatoes, cut into wedges

Italian dressing *enough to satisfy your own personal level of dressedness*

4 ounces crumbled blue cheese (about 1 cup)

2 to 3 tablespoons really good extra virgin olive oil

Preheat the grill to medium-high. If using a broiler, start it heating here as well. **Season** the steaks well with salt and pepper. **Grill** the steak to the desired doneness. I cook steaks in the 1- to 1½-inch-thick range for about 5 minutes per side, and that usually gives me a nice medium-rare. I use a hot grill, and pretty much turn the steaks over only once. If you're using a broiler, make sure it's well heated and then get the steaks close to the broiler—no more than a couple of inches away—and cook for about the same time as on a grill. **Remove** the steaks from the grill and cover with foil. Allow to rest for about 10 minutes. **Toss** the greens lightly with the tomatoes and dressing and divide among 4 plates. **Slice** the steak thinly across the grain on an angle and place on top of the salad. Top with the blue cheese crumbles, drizzle with the olive oil, and serve.

Note: The cold-steak version of this salad is best made by just throwing an extra steak on the grill one night and serving it sliced thin in the salad the next day.

Specify the Brand of Alcohol You Want at a Bar or Restaurant

In many places, just asking for a scotch and soda, or vodka on the rocks will get you the worst possible rotgut alcohol known to man. Learn what's good and what you like—then ask for it.

Day-After Stuffing Omelet

Makes 1 omelet

You're laughing, right? "A stuffing omelet? This guy's a nut job!" Well it was invented with my nephews Marc and Troy one après-Thanksgiving morning and I don't think you want to call my nephews nutjobs. . . or do you? I'm serious about how good this is, so don't laugh until you've tried it. But it's pretty much a twice-a-year event—and requires leftover stuffing, which is the perfect reason to make extra.

3 large eggs *you've heard of the 2-egg omelet? Well, this is its 3-egg cousin*

½ tablespoon butter

⅓ cup (approximately) leftover stuffing, at room temp

1 slice American cheese *you can use any kind you like, but American really makes it and melts beautifully*

Beat the eggs well in a bowl. In a nonstick pan over medium heat, **melt** the butter, **pour** in the eggs, and allow to **"set"**— the key here is not to disturb the bottom layer of the eggs. Gently pull the eggs away from the edges of the pan about an inch at a time, allowing the uncooked eggs to run behind. Do this all the way around the pan. When it starts to look pretty set, **add** the stuffing to one half, cover with the cheese, and flip the other side over, making a half-moon, and cook till done. **Put** on a plate, enjoy, and wait for next year.

Note: For a simpler version you could always just do this as a scrambled egg sort of thing.

It's really easy to fall into the habit of serving the same things all the time. If you wouldn't wear the same clothes everyday, why eat the same food everyday?

Mac and (Blue) Cheese with Bacon

Serves 8

This is the trifecta of all my favorite foods in one dish—sautéed onions, bacon, and blue cheese—all surrounded by cheesy mac and topped with crunchy panko crumbs. What kryptonite was to Superman, this is to me. It is my one true weakness. If I make it, I eat it—all of it. Damn, it's so good.

1 package Kraft® Deluxe Macaroni & Cheese Dinner
I didn't say you had to start from scratch, did I? **(see Note)**

½ tablespoon olive oil

¾ cup yellow onion, diced small

One 2-ounce pack "ready bacon," chopped small

4 ounces blue cheese, crumbled

4 tablespoons (½ stick) butter

1½ cups panko crumbs (Japanese bread crumbs available in the supermarket Asian foods aisle)

Preheat the oven to 350°F. **Make** the macaroni according to the package directions. While it's cooking, **add** the oil to a nonstick skillet over medium heat, then add the onion and cook, stirring occasionally, until softened, about 5 minutes. **Add** the bacon near the end, to crisp it up, and cook about 3 more minutes. **Add** the onion-bacon mixture and the blue cheese to the finished mac and **mix** together well. **Place** in a buttered ovenproof casserole dish—about a 9 × 9–inch should be fine. **Melt** the remaining butter and mix with the panko crumbs. **Sprinkle** the mixture on top of the mac. **Bake** until the top is brown and crispy, 20 to 25 minutes.

Note: *There are different types of Kraft macaroni and cheese; this is the "deluxe" box with the squeeze pouch of cheese, NOT the powdered stuff.*

Specify What to Bring to a Potluck

A potluck is my absolute very favorite kind of party to go to. Everyone brings the one thing they make best. But a successful potluck requires two things:

1. The guests should come from a variety of different ethnic backgrounds—trust me, the food will be way better. If the only people you invite are 35-year-old guys from New Jersey, the food might be good but it will all be the same.

2. You must assign the categories. We had a beach potluck years ago for a retiring co-worker and because it was left to everyone to bring what they wanted, we ended up with eight cold pasta salads (and I hate cold pasta salads). Even the people who like them hated them by the end of the day.

My Mom's
Lox Dip

Makes about 1½ cups

So simple yet so delicious. Man, my mom is good.

4 ounces sliced lox, chopped fine

4 ounces cream cheese, softened

3 tablespoons mayonnaise

4 green onions (scallions), white and light green
parts only, chopped fine (save some for garnish)

1 hard-boiled egg, grated

Freshly ground black pepper

Toasted Pitas (page 63), for serving

Combine the lox, cream cheese, mayo, 3 of the chopped green onions, egg, and pepper to taste in a bowl and mix well. Put on a serving plate and **top** with extra green onion. **Serve** with the Toasted Pitas.

Note: *You can make this in advance, which is totally cool—just don't serve it too cool, know what I mean?*

Lox is thinly sliced salmon that's been smoked & cured. I'm Jewish and grew up with it. In fact I call it the "food of my people" which is not really accurate, but lox tastes really good. If you haven't had it, go get some.

Lemon Pasta with Mint

Serves 6

My sister-in-law Sandy (we call her Auntie Sandy) turned me on to this simple little deal. This is to the pasta world what the little black dress is to the fashion world—simple and elegant. Nice analogy, huh? I'm an idiot.

1 pound pasta *whatever kind of pasta you feel like*

4 tablespoons (½ stick) butter

Juice of 1 lemon, plus the grated zest

Kosher salt and freshly ground black pepper

Grated Parmesan cheese

3 tablespoons finely chopped fresh mint

In a large pot of boiling water, **cook** the pasta according to the directions on the box. When the pasta is almost done, **melt** the butter in a medium pot with the lemon juice and **mix** well. **Drain** the pasta and put in the pot with the butter and lemon juice and add salt and pepper to taste. **Toss** everything together. Put on serving plates and **top** each with some Parmesan, a little lemon zest, and the mint.

By the way, ravioli is a great thing to use here.

Pour yourself a Lager and

Outside
Food

Lime, bust out your favorite Bermudas (shorts, that is), push aside your Adirondack (low-riding wooden chair that belongs in Cape Cod, that is), and get busy in the great outdoors. That would be "**get busy**" in the cooking sense, not in the "what people do behind closed doors" sense. But you know, if it were really nice out, you could always … I think I'll stop now.

Lager and Lime
Tomato and
Gazpacho
Stuffed Burgers
Super Simple
Teriyaki and
Grilled Eggplant
Sandwich
Burgers Pesto

Red Beer
Yellow Pepper
Grilled Lobster
Maple Chops
Mango Salsa
Bacon Scallops
Parmesan
No-Bun Lamb
BBQ Shrimp

Beer Two Ways

Lager and Lime

Makes 1

The Brits mix lager with Rose's lime juice to make a refreshingly different drink. This is really great in the summer. Sidle up to the bar and give it a go.

Food consumed outside calls for beer consumed outside, doesn't it? Here are two things I like to do to make them a little different.

1 bottle beer, preferably a good lager
2 tablespoons Rose's lime juice

Open the bottle and take a big sip. **Replace** the big sip with the lime juice and then, with your thumb over the top, **turn** the bottle upside down to mix, then turn back and slowly release your thumb—carbonation, you know . . . **Enjoy**.

Grilling, if it wasn't obvious,

is about the heat, so first make sure your grill is really hot. If you can hold your hand about 3 inches above the grates for more than 3 seconds, it ain't ready, so shut the lid and go check your e-mail.

Red Beer

Serves 2

Matt, my drinking partner . . . I mean, neighbor . . . is a big fan of this. It's a nice change if you can get your head around the beer and tomato juice combo.

One 12-ounce flavorful beer (nothing "light")
6 ounces spicy tomato juice
2 teaspoons Worcestershire sauce
Kosher salt and freshly ground black pepper to taste
2 big fat lime wedges

Divide all of the ingredients (except for the limes) between 2 glasses and mix well. **Squeeze** the lime juice into each glass and then drop in the wedges. **Drink**. Have another.

Tomato and Yellow Pepper Gazpacho

Serves 6

I know what you're thinking: cold soup is a foo-foo dainty little thing that belongs at a ladies' garden party. Don't be hatin'—this is the perfect outside food that's big, full of flavor, and deserves to be made. Throw everything in a food processor, and you're a genius. I like to grill a bunch of huge shrimp to serve alongside this.

2 yellow bell peppers, seeded and cut into big chunks

4 ripe medium-sized tomatoes, quartered and seeded

2 medium-sized cucumbers, peeled, split lengthwise, seeds scooped out, and cut into big chunks

½ large yellow onion, cut into big chunks

3 cloves garlic

2 tablespoons hot sauce *I like Cholula hot sauce, which is actually as readily available as your beloved Tabasco*

1 cup fresh cilantro *save a little for garnish*

4 ounces Bloody Mary mix, if you have it *or tomato juice would be just fine*

Kosher salt and freshly ground black pepper to taste

The key is to **blend** everything, so if you can fit everything in the food processor the first time, go ahead and blend until smooth but still a bit chunky. If you need to, do it in **2** shifts— eventually everything will fit for a final whiz. But don't mix too much—**chunky** is the way to go. **Serve** with a little finely chopped cilantro on top.

Cooking Outdoors

Why is it that most things cooked outside just taste better? Is it the air that does it? Or that if you're out there cooking, the weather's usually nicer? Whatever it is, it just works with pretty much everything. Grilled cheese on the stove, nice, but standard. Grilled cheese on the BBQ, amazing. Hot dogs cooked in a pan, okay. Hot dogs grilled in the glorious out-of-doors—fantastico. Asparagus boiled in a pot inside—limp and boring. Asparagus drizzled with a little olive oil and grilled over the open flame—majestic. (For the record, asparagus *can* be cooked beautifully inside, but they need to be roasted in the oven.) Your grandmother's liver, cheese, and broccoli casserole...well, maybe not everything works.

Grilled **Lobster**

Serves 4

There's this big mystique about lobster. People think because it's stupidly expensive and hard to get, that it's also stupidly hard to cook. But it's no more difficult to cook than a burger—okay, make that an expensive burger. But every so often it's nice to bust out some lobster for a special occasion. And my way is easy, as there is no lobster wrangling or death involved—I use just the tails.

8 tablespoons (1 stick) butter

2 tablespoons chili powder

2 cloves garlic, chopped fine

4 lobster tails

Heat the grill to medium-high. **Mix** the butter, chili powder, and garlic in a small pot over low heat until melted and well blended. **Reserve** half of the butter mixture for serving and bring the rest to the grillside for basting. With a pair of really good kitchen shears, **cut** up through the middle of the shell toward the tail, but stop before the tail. Then, with a knife, cut down through the lobster to the bottom shell plate, but not through the plate. Pick up the tail in both hands and **fold** back the sides—like you're opening a book, exposing all the lobster meat. Now **brush** the exposed lobster meat really well with the butter mixture and place, meat side down, on the grill for about

5 minutes, then **turn** and cook for another 4 to 5 minutes, or until fully cooked through, basting often with the butter mixture. **Serve** with the reserved butter mixture.

What To Do When You Burned What You're Grilling

Start by staying calm, because if you freak, your guests will know for sure to expect the worst. You need to first determine the degree of ruinedness, so make a small cut and have a look. Even though the outside may look totally charred, if there's even a little color left in the middle, here's what to do:

> Bring it inside, smiling at your guests but saying nothing—this is not the time for honesty.

> Slice it thinly across the grain—this will not only help make it more tender, but more importantly will minimize the amount of burned outside you'd get in each bite.

> If it's worse than better, a disguise may be in order. I would suggest plating the thin slices and then covering them with something. A salsa is always a good idea (and easy to keep in the pantry). Blue cheese crumbles and a good drizzle of olive oil make a delicious and more sophisticated topping. Either will usually keep your guests from becoming too suspicious.

Stuffed Burgers

Makes 4 burgers

I love these. To your guests they'll just look like big fat burgers—but you'll know there's a surprise waiting inside.

1 tablespoon olive oil

1 small red onion, thinly sliced

Kosher salt and freshly ground black pepper

4 slices cheese *call me crazy, but, again, I like American slices here; it's all about the meltability*

Eight ¼-pound burgers *the already formed guys from the store are ideal for this*

½ cup steak sauce *try a spicy one*

4 hamburger buns, lettuce, tomato *blah blah blah . . . must I suggest everything?*

Preheat the grill to high. **Add** the oil to a nonstick skillet over medium heat, add the onion, season with salt and pepper, and cook, stirring, until nicely softened and starting to brown,

Don't plan on grilling the same day you buy a new BBQ. I've done it and ended up at the neighbors' for dinner. In fact, even the same week is a little questionable. Aways look for the "we'll build it for you" option when buying a new grill.

about 5 minutes. Set aside. **Place** a slice of cheese on 4 of the patties, then some of the onions, then some steak sauce, and top with the other patty. Gently **pinch** the edges of the 2 burgers together to seal in the filling, and you're ready. Turn the grill down to medium and **cook** the burgers on both sides until they're the way you like them. This will take approximately 7 to 10 minutes a side—remember, you're cooking 2 patties. **Bun** them up, and away you go . . .

Note: Use your imagination next time with different stuffing items: blue cheese, roasted peppers, Cap'n Crunch. It's all good.

Maple Chops

Serves 4

This uses maple syrup, but if you don't have that, you can use pancake syrup. If you don't have pancake syrup . . .what? You don't have pancake syrup? What's going on in your house?

1 cup maple syrup

4 tablespoons soy sauce

2 fat cloves garlic, chopped fine

4 pork chops, bone in or out *I like it in*

In a resealable bag, **combine** the syrup, soy sauce, and garlic and mix well. **Marinate** the chops in ¾ of the syrup–soy sauce mixture (reserving the rest for basting) for as long as you have—from 1 hour up to overnight. **Preheat** the grill to high. **Grill** the chops until done, about 10 to 12 minutes total, **basting** well with the reserved sauce during cooking. Crispy outside and tender inside—that's your goal.

Size totally matters—give yourself a chance and leave the thin little piece of meat your supermarket has deemed "perfect for the grill" at the supermarket. Buy your steaks at least an inch to an inch-and-a-half thick.

Super Simple Mango Salsa

Makes about 2½ cups

This makes even the simplest grilled pork, chicken, or fish fantastic. Just serve it on the side, on the top, or even under something, and you'll be fine.

2 ripe mangos, peeled, pitted, and diced small

½ cup red onion, diced small

¼ cup finely chopped fresh cilantro

1 lime, zested and juiced *that means the outside* **and** *inside*

1 tablespoon finely chopped fresh ginger

¼ teaspoon cayenne pepper

Kosher salt and freshly ground black pepper to taste

Combine the mango, onion, cilantro, lime zest, lime juice, ginger, and cayenne in a bowl (not a metal one), mix well, and you're done. *Okay, fine.* **Season** well with the salt and pepper, mix well, and now you're done, but let stand for at least 20 minutes before serving. You can make this up to a couple of hours in advance, **cover**, and **refrigerate**. *Scout's honor—this makes almost anything grilled fantastic.* Now you're **done**.

Teriyaki and Bacon Scallops

Makes 12

You're probably tired of me telling you that there are things you should keep in your freezer for last-minute appetite suppression. Scallops are one of them because they freeze really well and defrost quickly. Sea scallops are the big ones, and bay scallops are the little guys. This recipe uses the big boys.

1 pound sea scallops, should be about 12

12 slices "ready bacon" *the already cooked and ready-to-go kind*

3 long metal skewers or 3 long wooden ones (soaked in water about 30 minutes)

½ cup teriyaki sauce

1 tablespoon toasted sesame seeds

Preheat the BBQ or grill pan on high. **Wrap** each scallop with a slice of bacon and skewer (4 to a skewer). Make sure they stay tightly wrapped. **Spray** the BBQ or grill pan with nonstick spray and lay down the skewers. **Don't** move 'em. Let them **cook** for 3 to 4 minutes, until really good grill marks develop, then **flip** over. **Brush** the now-cooked tops with sauce and grill the second side for 2 to 3 more minutes, or until that side looks equally as cool. **Remove** and brush them once more with the sauce. Put on a serving plate and **sprinkle** with sesame seeds before serving.

Grilled Eggplant Parmesan Sandwich

Serves 4

Back in the day, eggplant Parmesan meant breaded, deep-fried, and artery-clogging. Well, guess what? We're not back in the day anymore, so we're going all easy and all delicious.

1 medium globe eggplant, sliced into eight
 1/3-inch slices

3 tablespoons olive oil

Kosher salt and freshly ground black pepper

1 cup shredded Parmesan cheese

2 large ripe tomatoes, sliced into eight
 1/3-inch slices

4 crusty Italian-type rolls, split in half

1 bunch fresh basil

Preheat the grill to medium-high. **Brush** the eggplant and tomatoes with the olive oil and season with salt and pepper. **Grill** the eggplant on both sides, 3 to 5 minutes a side, until soft and marked with grill lines. **Add** the cheese to 4 of the eggplant slices when you flip them and it will melt as the other side cooks. Put the tomatoes on the grill, but only for about 2 minutes on each side. **Remove** the tomatoes and quickly toast the buns facedown on the hot grill, then remove. **Build** them like this: One slice of eggplant without cheese, 2 slices of tomato, 3 large basil leaves, and top with the second eggplant slice with the melted cheese. **Place** the roll top on, slice in half, and eat. You can **thank me** later.

No-Bun Lamb Burgers

Serves 4

Aristotle Onassis, move the hell over—I'm in control of all things Greek now. You might have to look a bit in the market for the ground lamb, but it's probably there. You'll love these, and if there were ever a time to go without a bun, this would be it.

1½ pounds ground lamb

⅓ cup finely chopped fresh mint

⅓ cup yellow onion, diced small

Kosher salt and freshly ground black pepper

4 ounces feta cheese, in a block

Extra virgin olive oil, for drizzling *if it's Greek, excellent; if not, the burger will never know*

Preheat the grill to high. In a bowl, **mix** all of the ingredients together except the feta cheese and oil. **Shape** into 4 patties. **Make** a hole in the side of each patty, jam a 1 × 1–inch block of the cheese into the middle of each, and seal the edges around it. **Grill** until they're cooked the way you like them, but please don't dry them out. **Serve** with a good decent drizzle of good olive oil—and maybe a salad.

Pesto
BBQ Shrimp

Makes 24 skewers

Everyone loves eating off a stick—and you can easily whip these out at a moment's notice for a group. Plus they require only two ingredients—okay, technically three, if you count the stick. Larger shrimp are better—like at least 21/25s. That means there are between 21 and 25 shrimp per pound. I like to pile them on a bitchin'-looking platter and serve them along with cocktails.

24 large shrimp, deveined with the shell and tail removed

24 long wooden skewers (soaked in water for about 30 minutes)

1 cup premade pesto *store-bought is just fine*

Thread shrimp onto each skewer, lengthwise. **Coat** both sides of the shrimp well with the pesto and let sit for about 15 minutes. Reserve some pesto for serving. **Preheat** the grill to high. **Grill** for a couple of minutes on each side and serve with a little extra pesto.

Remember that dumb old

Seafood

joke "I'm on a seafood diet. I 'see' food and I eat it"? Maybe it's not so dumb. And when the food tastes like this, it's even less **dumb**. This would be the perfect time to read my thinking on things like frozen shrimp in the Basic Stuff to Know section.

Chili Salmon
That Works on
or Almost Any
Shrimpy Seared
Ginger Scallops
Salmon Mahimahi
Old-School

Something Great
Halibut, Sea Bass,
Big White Fish
Tuna Burger
Cedar Plank
with Salsa Cream
Curried Shrimp

Chili **Salmon**

Serves 4

Quickly seared salmon—crispy on the top and moist in the middle, with a hint of heat. Damn!

Four 8-ounce salmon fillets, *the skin-on-the-bottom kind*

Kosher salt and freshly ground black pepper

6 tablespoons chili oil *found in the Asian foods section of most supermarkets*

1 cup finely chopped green onions (scallions), white and light green parts only

With the skin side down, **season** the salmon well with salt and pepper and cover with the chili oil. Let sit for 15 minutes. **Preheat** a nonstick skillet really, really well over high heat until almost smoking. Carefully **add** the salmon, skin side up this time. Shake the pan a little to keep the salmon from sticking, and let cook—depending on how thick your salmon is, it should not take more than 5 minutes. You're essentially looking for a nicely browned and starting-to-get-crispy surface—the salmon, that is, not the pan. **Flip** over and cook another 3 to 5 minutes. Remove to serving plates and completely cover with the green onions. *It will be beautiful and amazingly tastiful (good word, huh?), but not too spicy.*

Something Great That Works on Halibut, Sea Bass, or Almost Any Big White Fish

Serves 4

Shortly after I started my show, I received a recipe from viewer Ray. And though I changed it a bit, I thank him for his recipe.

1½ pounds sea bass or halibut, cut into 4 even pieces and with the skin removed

Kosher salt and freshly ground black pepper

2 tablespoons Asian-style sesame oil

2 tablespoons butter

1 nice-sized ripe tomato *not mushy***, diced small**

1 to 2 tablespoons freshly grated Parmesan cheese

⅓ cup finely chopped fresh cilantro

Preheat the oven to 425°F. **Season** the fish with salt and pepper and rub with the sesame oil. **Heat** an ovenproof pan over medium heat until hot, then add the fish. Sear for 3 to 4 minutes on one side—it's going into the oven, so you won't need to flip it. **Put** the butter in a small bowl and melt it in the microwave. **Add** the tomato, Parmesan, and cilantro and mix well. **Remove** the pan from the stove top, **cover** the top of the fish with the tomato mixture, and place the pan in the oven until cooked through, about 5 minutes. **Serve** immediately.

Shrimpy

Serves 4 to 6

This is the best sharing recipe ever. We had it the first time with our friends Bruno and Jill. In fact, Jill has a sheet pan of mine she refuses to give back. The idea is that each couple gets their own pan of these to eat. You dip good bread in it, peel the shells and throw them on the newspaper tablecloth you've made, drink some beer—it's the night of nights. But there's no way to pass this off as anything but a recipe with an assload of butter and pepper. Healthy? Are you nuts? Good? Absofrickinlutely. Just don't have it every night of the week.

2 pounds (8 sticks) butter, thinly sliced

6 tablespoons finely chopped garlic

2 pounds raw large shrimp *31/40s work well* **deveined but not peeled**

8 tablespoons freshly ground black pepper

Sourdough bread, for serving

Preheat the oven to broil. Dividing the ingredients evenly between two 9 × 13–inch pans, spread out a quarter of the sliced butter and top with a quarter of the garlic, all of the shrimp, and half the pepper. Then top with the remaining garlic, butter, and pepper. Broil until the shrimp are nicely pink, about 10 minutes—you shouldn't need to flip them. Serve with lots of warm, crusty sourdough bread for dipping—lots.

Seared Tuna Burger

Makes 4 burgers

There are hamburgers, turkey burgers, chicken burgers, and even tofu burgers—so why not a tuna burger?

¼ cup mayo

2 tablespoons small capers, drained

2 tablespoons diced red onion

Juice of ½ lemon *no seeds, please*

Four 6-ounce yellowfin tuna steaks
  even the frozen ones make for a great burger

2 tablespoons olive oil

Kosher salt and freshly ground black pepper

4 buns *I'll leave it up to you, but please, something kinda cool—preferably not your everyday plain hamburger bun*

Red leaf lettuce

Preheat the grill to medium-high. (You can also cook these in a nonstick pan on the stove top.) **Combine** the mayo, capers, onion, and lemon juice in a small bowl, mix well, and set aside. Lightly **drizzle** both sides of the tuna with the oil and season with salt and pepper on both sides. **Place** the tuna on the grill. **Cook** quickly until both sides are seared and nicely browned—maybe 1½ to 2 minutes per side—but still a little pink in the middle. You can see the fish change color as it cooks. When the color changes about ¼ of the way through one side, I **flip** it and do the same on the other. This will leave a little pink in the middle. If you're so inclined, and I am, toast the buns. **Spread** on some of the sauce and top with the lettuce. **Place** the finished tuna fillet on top of one side of the bun, cover with a top bun, and go to town—okay, that's just an expression. Don't actually go anywhere, just eat it.

Ginger **Scallops**

Makes 4 servings of 3 scallops each, *or 3 servings of 4 each,*

or 2 servings of 6 each, or... you get the idea

I can remember the day I figured out how **not** to turn scallops into hockey pucks. Once you get it, you'll want to make them all the time. The key is simple: a lot of heat and very little cooking. Just think of this: you can eat them raw, so why cook them for three hours in a pan? See Scallop 101 on the next page.

12 large sea scallops, about 1 pound

2 tablespoons butter, softened

1½ tablespoons finely chopped fresh ginger

1½ tablespoons finely chopped green onions (scallions), white and light green parts only

1 tablespoon peanut oil

Dry the scallops by laying them out on a paper towel and setting them aside while you deal with the other ingredients. **Mix** together the butter, ginger, and green onions well in a small bowl and set aside. **Preheat** a nonstick skillet over high heat for a couple of minutes. (If it starts to smoke, just pull it off for 15 to 20 seconds.) Then **add** ½ tablespoon of the oil. It will probably start smoking—that's okay. Just add half the scallops and sear until nicely browned, about 2 minutes.

If you cook too many scallops at a time, they'll steam instead of sear, and that's bad.

Turn them and sear the second side until they're just about ready to come off the heat, about another 2 minutes. **Add** half of the ginger-butter to the skillet and make sure the scallops get well coated by turning them. **Remove** to serving plates, drizzle with any of the remaining pan butter, and serve. **Repeat** with the remaining scallops.

Scallop 101

The cool thing about scallops is that if your heat is high enough, the scallops will be ready to flip when they look beautifully browned on the bottom side—you can totally use that as a gauge for cooking time. When I make something like this, which cooks quickly but has to be done in batches, I serve the first batch and tell the recipients to start eating, and not to wait for the rest to be served. Political correctness be damned. It's about the food, baby!

Cedar Plank Salmon

Serves 6

For me, this might just be the Holy Grail of recipes—easy, with only three main ingredients, totally impressive looking, and it tastes amazing.

1 cedar plank *the dimensions are up to you, but get one at least an inch wider and a few inches longer than the salmon you're using, and then make sure it'll fit your BBQ; see Note*

1 whole salmon fillet, 2 to 2½ pounds, skin on or off *it's no big deal either way*

1 tablespoon olive oil

Kosher salt and freshly ground black pepper

2 cups brown sugar, approximately

Soak the plank in water for 1 to 2 hours. **Preheat** the grill to high for at least 15 minutes with the lid closed. **Place** the salmon on the plank and rub the top with the olive oil. Season really well with salt and pepper. **Cover**—and I mean **cover**—with the brown sugar so you no longer see salmon peeking through. **Place** on the grill and **shut** the lid. It'll **cook** 10 to 20 minutes total. I know that's a wide range, but it completely depends on your grill and the salmon. You're looking for a medium-rare salmon, but the problem is you can't really push on it like you can with a piece of meat to see if it's ready, because the melting sugar will burn the $%#@ out of your finger.

Peek as little as possible, but have a spray bottle of water at the ready because we're cooking wood here, and the chances of flames are pretty high.

When it's finished, carefully **remove** the plank from the grill and let the plank finish smoking outside before you bring it in your house.

I serve it right on the plank—but remember to put something under it, as it'll be very sooty.

Note: *You can get cedar planks in almost any cookware store, but usually, they're thin, expensive, and small. I buy untreated 6-foot cedar planks—1 inch thick and 8 inches wide—at a local lumberyard and just cut them into the size I need.*

If I cook fish in the oven, I broil it. I don't like to bake it. I find it stays moister when I broil it. Wait, that doesn't sound right... I find it stays way frickin' moister. That's better.

Mahimahi with Salsa Cream

Serves 6

If I told you we were having mahimahi with hot sour cream, you'd probably go, "Eewwwww." But every time I make it, the reaction is the same: "Holy crap!" You can't argue with that.

1 red bell pepper, diced small

1 yellow bell pepper, diced small

1 Anaheim chile pepper, diced small

or a regular green pepper will do

½ tablespoon olive oil

Kosher salt and freshly ground pepper

6 mahimahi filets, about 8 ounces each

1 cup sour cream

1 cup salsa verde (green salsa)

2 tablespoons finely chopped fresh cilantro

Cook the red, yellow, and chile peppers in a nonstick skillet with the oil over medium-high heat, stirring occasionally, until softened, 5 to 6 minutes, and set aside. **Season** the fish well with salt and pepper. **Heat** a nonstick pan with a little oil, and sear the fish on each side until nicely browned and cooked the way you want it, which is probably somewhere about 5 minutes per side. While the fish cooks, **combine** the sour cream and salsa in a little pot over medium heat until

it gets bubbly. **Plate** the whole deal by putting some of the mixed peppers on a plate, the mahimahi on the peppers, and spoon some of the salsa cream over the top. **Garnish** with a little chopped cilantro and serve.

Warning

I'm totally in favor of subbing food items when you don't have what a recipe calls for. In fact, I encourage it. But, and this is a big *but* . . . this recipe calls for green salsa, and I'm here to say that if you use red salsa instead, this will become one of the most horrifyingly ugly dishes you've ever made and will look like something that rhymes with "duke." So don't.

Old-School Curried Shrimp

Serves 6

The food memory is an amazing thing. You can eat something that instantly takes you to another time. This takes me to when I was ten years old . . . at home . . . my mom in the kitchen . . . my dad watching Walter Cronkite . . . and my brothers trying to stuff my head into the toilet . . . too much . . . This is the perfect "cold-weather, sitting-in-front-of-the-fire-and-watching-a-great-movie" kind of food. Puff pastry shells overflowing with a fabulously fragrant curry. So great.

1 package frozen puff pastry shells
if you don't know these, get it together

4 tablespoons (½ stick) butter, melted

¼ cup flour

2 teaspoons curry powder

½ teaspoon paprika

1½ cups milk, whole *or 2 percent is fine*

1½ cups cooked tiny "bay" shrimp

3 tablespoons ketchup

¼ cup dry sherry

Kosher salt and freshly ground black pepper

Thaw and **cook** the puff pastry shells according to package directions. In a small pot over medium heat, **melt** the butter, **add** the flour, curry, and paprika, and **stir** to combine. It will be a thick, dry paste. Slowly **stir** in the milk and allow to thicken, about 5 minutes. **Add** the shrimp, ketchup, and sherry and heat through. **Add** salt and pepper to taste. **Spoon** the mixture into the puff pasty shells and serve.

Note: You're gonna read this recipe, see the ketchup part, and think I'm a nut job. I'm not—it's my mother's recipe, so you'd be calling her a nut job. Want to rethink it?

Have you read my thoughts on frozen shrimp in the Basic Stuff to Know section (page 5)? If not, go read them. If you have, never mind and good for you.

When it's **_no bueno_**

The Weather Blows, But the Food Doesn't

outside, you've gotta go for something slightly more substantial for your soul—and anything on this list will fit the bill. This is not the time for some wispy little nothing-of-a-dish. Go for it!

Tomato Beef Home Meatballs Tomatoes and Spaghetti with Cheese Spicy-ish Meatball Strogy Double

Chow Mein Motor Pasta with Mascarpone Spinach and Blue Sausage Pasta Meatball Sands Ballpark Dogs

Tomato Beef Chow Mein

Serves 6

There's an unwritten kinship between the Jews and the Chinese—I don't know why, there just is. Growing up in Vancouver, Canada, I spent every Sunday night with my family at a Chinese restaurant, and my Uncle Bob would always be the one to order. He was like the "King of Chinese Food." This dish was always in the lineup, and we loved it—though I'm pretty certain they didn't use instant ramen noodles. Black bean sauce is pretty fantastic, and you can get it in the Asian foods section of most supermarkets.

2 packages instant ramen noodles
the cup or plastic-bag kind

1 pound steak *you choose, but*
I like a New York steak for this

½ tablespoon peanut oil

4 ripe medium-sized tomatoes,
cut into 8 wedges each

2 tablespoons black bean sauce

1 tablespoon water

Cook the noodles according to the package directions. For the Styrofoam type, I just fill the cup with water, microwave for 2 minutes, then drain well. For the plastic-bag kind, I boil the noodles without the seasoning packet, then drain them well. **Slice** the steak very thinly. **Preheat** a large skillet or wok really well over medium heat, then **add** the oil. When the oil is smoking—and not until—add the beef and tomatoes, and **stir-fry** for a couple minutes until the beef changes color and is cooked through, 3 to 4 minutes. In a small bowl, **mix** the black bean sauce with the water and set aside. **Add** the drained noodles and black bean sauce to the beef and tomato mixture and stir the whole business until the flavor is through everything and all is heated. Then **serve**.

There's no question that crappy weather food is worse for you than fair weather food, but who cares really? That's why they sell those big, bulky sweaters in the winter, isn't it?

Motor Home Meatballs

Makes about 20 small meatballs

My friend Peter's mom makes these. But let me put it this way: they're probably not appropriate for the "big dinner" when the boss comes over. But some beers, a little football, these—and you're golden.

1 pound lean ground beef

2 tablespoons olive oil

1 cup grape jelly *yes, grape jelly*

1 cup chili sauce *the ketchupy kind in the condiment aisle, not the Thai kind sold in Asian markets*

Roll the ground beef into balls *well, what am I supposed to call them?* **Preheat** a nonstick skillet over medium heat. **Cook** the meatballs in the olive oil until browned on all sides, about 5 minutes. In a pot large enough to later hold the meatballs, **combine** the jelly and chili sauce. **Add** the browned meatballs to the sauce and simmer over lowish heat until cooked through, 15 to 20 minutes.

If you make the balls small enough you can do the toothpick thing for serving, but I like them on a bowl of steamy rice, maybe with a sprinkle of sesame seeds on top.

Note: If you can roll 20 meatballs, you can roll 40. I say you make a double batch, brown them all, and then throw half in the freezer. Then, the next time you want this dish, you're most of the way there. Just mix the sauce, put the meatballs in the pot still frozen, and let them simmer a little longer to thaw and cook through.

Pasta with Tomatoes and Mascarpone

Serves 6

If mascarpone cheese were bedsheets, it would be the equivalent of about 10,000 thread count—smooth, silky, and completely over-the-top luxurious. I know that's a ridiculous comparison, but who cares? Technically, mascarpone is a triple cream cheese that works beautifully in all kinds of things, including this recipe. My friend Sue makes this all the time, and it's so good and easy. She doesn't watch my show, but that's okay. A guy can't have everything, right?

1 pound pasta *gnocchi is nice for this*

1 tablespoon olive oil

½ large yellow onion, diced

1 clove garlic, chopped fine

One 28-ounce can whole peeled tomatoes

1 cup (about 8 ounces) mascarpone cheese

Fresh basil, chopped fine for garnish

Bring a large pot of water to a boil, add the pasta, and cook according to the package directions. While the pasta cooks, add the oil to a nonstick skillet over medium heat, then add the onion and garlic and cook, stirring, until tender, about 5 minutes. Drain the tomatoes and add to the onion, squishing them with the back of a spoon to break them up. Mix well and allow to heat through for a few minutes. Add the cheese, **stir** well, and allow to cook slowly, stirring often, for about 5 minutes until all is thick, silky, and creamy. **Drain** the pasta in a colander, add to the sauce, and **mix** everything together. **Transfer** the pasta to serving plates, top with the chopped basil, and serve.

Feeding Kids

I'm always surprised to hear parents say "My kids would **never** eat that." These are also the same parents who say "My 5-year-old will just not go to bed before 10 pm." The basic concept is that we as the adults need to take the lead—for bed and food. My kids will eat almost anything—ok, my kids will at least **TRY** almost anything and will eat most things. But that's because I started them young. You probably have as much of a chance changing your 14-year-old's taste in food as you do changing their taste in music. "Hey, Billy, I know you really like that Eminem CD, but how about trying a little 5TH Dimension. They were really big in my day..." And sometimes you might even need a little white lie to accomplish the mission. My youngest really liked chicken when he was little, and when we wanted him to try something new, we just called it chicken. "Here honey, want some more lamb, I mean chicken?" Get the idea? If I said I didn't like something I'd never had when I was a kid, my mom would say, "How do you know?" and it always took the wind out of my sails. So start them young at trying different foods—it will only end up being a good thing. And by the way, 5-year-olds should not go to bed at 10 pm, really.

Spaghetti with Spinach and Blue Cheese

Serves 6

You can bust this out in less than fifteen minutes—and that includes waiting for the water to boil. But go for the glory and let them think you've been working your tail off all day.

1 pound spaghetti

4 ounces blue cheese, crumbled

4 tablespoons olive oil

3 cloves garlic, chopped fine

½ teaspoon red pepper flakes

One 7-ounce bag "ready-to-go" fresh
   spinach leaves

Bring a large pot of water to a **boil**. Add the spaghetti, and **cook** until still slightly firm (a minute or two less than what is specified on the package). While the spaghetti cooks, put the blue cheese, olive oil, garlic, and pepper flakes in a bowl, **mix** well, and set aside. When the spaghetti is done, **add** the spinach to boiling water with the spaghetti to cook for about 15 seconds. Make sure it all gets submerged and mixed in well—it'll wilt really quickly. **Drain** the spaghetti and spinach well and return to the pot. **Add** the blue cheese stuff to the pot, mix well, then **serve**.

Spicy-ish
Sausage Pasta

Serves 6

It's hard to explain the creamy and delicious reaction that happens when all these ingredients come together. A dish of it microwaved the next day is even more kick-ass. What more can I say?

1 tablespoon olive oil

1 pound spicy Italian sausage (casings removed), meat crumbled

4 cloves garlic, chopped fine

1 cup heavy whipping cream

1 pound pasta *any tube-shaped one will do; they hold the sauce better*

½ cup freshly grated Parmesan cheese

3 tablespoons butter

2 tablespoons finely chopped fresh Italian parsley *the flat kind*

Freshly ground black pepper

Bring a large pot of water to a boil. **Preheat** a nonstick pan over medium heat. **Add** the oil to the hot pan, then add the sausage and garlic. **Break** apart the sausage and cook, stirring occasionally, until it's no longer pink. Then add the cream and simmer over low heat. Add the pasta to the boiling water and **cook** according to the package instructions. When the pasta's ready, so is the sausage. **Drain** the pasta well in a colander and add to the sausage in the pan. Add the Parmesan, butter, and parsley, and **mix** well. To serve, **sprinkle** with a little more of the Parmesan cheese and season with pepper, and you're good. ***Really good.***

Meatball Strogy

Serves 6

Remember the good old days? Like when everyone thought it was cute that Michael Jackson had so many children as friends? Well, those days are gone, but the food doesn't have to be. This is so the perfect crappy-weather food, but it isn't a lot of work, as we've been led to believe. It goes from nothing to rich and luxuriously decadent in about fifteen minutes. Make a bunch of it and gather round an old episode of *Seinfeld*.

1 tablespoon olive oil

12 ounces fully cooked meatballs (about 24) from the supermarket, defrosted

½ cup diced yellow onion

One 12-ounce jar store-bought home-style beef gravy

½ cup sour cream

3 tablespoons fresh, finely chopped dill leaves

2 tablespoons prepared horseradish

12 ounces egg noodles, the wide ones

Preheat a large skillet over medium heat. Add the oil and onion, then add the meatballs, and **cook**, stirring occasionally, until nicely browned—should be less than 10 minutes. **Add** the gravy, sour cream, dill, and horseradish. Stir and heat through. **Cook** the noodles according to the package directions, drain, and **serve** with the M.B.S. on top.

Meatball
Sands

Serves 6

Once again, another frozen meatball item to the rescue. My editor said, "It isn't much of a recipe." That's funny because my dictionary defines a recipe as a "set of instructions for preparing a particular dish, including a list of the ingredients required." As far as I can tell, that's exactly what follows. And at 8:00 p.m. on a rainy, cold night, when you're dog-tired from a day of slaving at work, do you really want to reinvent the wheel? No. I think you just want the wheel to work, and this one works. These are gooey and messy— easy, but gooey, messy, and really awesome.

24 meatballs (about a pound), the smaller already-cooked and frozen guys

One 24-ounce jar of your favorite pasta sauce

6 crusty Italian rolls or buns

Hot sauce to taste

12 slices Provolone cheese

Just because I'm not a chef doesn't mean I don't steal their ideas. I use cheap plastic squeeze bottles for all kinds of things...different types of oil...chocolate syrup for cool plate decorating...water for flare-ups at the BBQ...anything you can think of.

Put the frozen meatballs and sauce in a pot and **simmer** over medium heat until the balls are cooked through, about 20 minutes. Meanwhile, **preheat** the broiler. When the meatballs are almost done, split the rolls down the middle, place them on a baking sheet, **toast** under the broiler very slightly, and remove. Put 4 of the meatballs plus some sauce on each roll, give a few good shakes with hot sauce, and cover each with 2 slices of cheese. Repeat with the remaining ingredients. Put the sandwiches back on the baking sheet, **set** under the broiler until the cheese has melted, and serve.

Double Ballpark Dogs

Serves 4

I realize hot dogs are usually nice-weather food, but these will smack any bad-weather day into submission. I don't know where the ballpark is that would serve these—but I want to go there, really bad.

8 hot dogs *go kosher; you'll thank me later*

1 tablespoon olive oil

1 smallish red onion, diced fine

One 2-ounce package "ready bacon," diced

One 14-ounce can chili *beans, no beans, meat, no meat—why would I care? You can use any kind of chili you want*

4 big sandwich rolls or big hot dog buns

Hot sauce to taste

½ cup shredded cheddar cheese

Preheat the broiler. Bring a pot of water to a **boil**, throw in the dogs, and cook until they start to "plump," 5 to 7 minutes. **Remove** the dogs from the pot and slice lengthwise down the center, but not all the way through—leave a little hinge. While the dogs cook, **preheat** a nonstick pan over medium heat. **Add** the oil and then the red onion and cook, stirring, until the onion softens really well, about 10 minutes. **Add** the bacon, cook, stirring occasionally, until the bacon crisps slightly, about 3 minutes more, and remove to a bowl. **Heat** the chili in a pot or the microwave—*it's up to you*. In the same pan you used for the onion and bacon, **sear** the dogs on both "open sides" until juicy, glistening, and starting to brown. Place the buns on a baking sheet and **toast** slightly under the broiler.

Build it like this:

Place 2 seared dogs on a lightly toasted bun, top with the chili, top with the onion and bacon mixture, top with a good few shakes of hot sauce, then top with some of the cheddar. **Repeat** with the remaining ingredients. **Place** the sandwiches back on the baking sheet and stick under the broiler until melty. *My bet is nothin' will top this.*

Try this for a bad weather cocktail, inspired by my friend Romaine: bourbon on the rocks with a splash of ginger ale, a big squeeze of lime, and a shake of bitters. Wait a minute, that's good in the summer, too. Oh well, I guess it's just good, period.

We often give vegetables a

Don't Be Mean to Vegetables

bad rap, and it seems to start when we're young. Kids dislike them, maybe from being forced to eat them, or maybe because of the "candy comparison" –their secret of measuring the value of something by "Would I rather have this or some candy?"

Even dogs hate most veggies—my dogs will eat anything that falls on the kitchen floor, but drop a piece of lettuce, and suddenly they're all picky. They're all over the back end of any stranger-dog that comes by, but get near some veggies . . . no way. So maybe we just need a little push to start eating vegetables again. And if you must ease your way into them, I'd start with the Cheese Garlic Fries—cuz they're not like eating veggies at all.

Cheese Garlic
Fajitas Painless
Favorite Way to
Roasted
Feta Not-Boiled
Chili Lime Corn
Veggies The Great
The Best Asparagus
Shiitakes Brussels
Actually Eat
(with Mint &

Fries Vegetable Risotto My Serve Artichokes Potatoes with Double Cabbage Great Grilled Potato Cake My Favorite Sprouts You'll Cucumber Soup Yogurt)

Cheese Garlic Fries

Serves 6, I think *But the thing is they're pretty darn good so you may end up eating them all by yourself, at which time they'd only serve 1. See my confusion?*

Bottom of the ninth, your team's up 9–8, and someone walks down the aisle to his seat and your nose follows him. It's those damn ballpark garlic fries. Well, here they are. No one who eats them doesn't like them, really. And they technically pass as veggies. Cool, huh?

One 28-ounce bag frozen shoestring French fries

3 tablespoons butter

6 cloves garlic, chopped fine

¼ cup freshly grated Parmesan cheese

3 tablespoons finely chopped fresh Italian parsley *the flat kind*

Kosher salt

Make the fries according to the package directions but make sure they get crispy. During the last 5 minutes of the fries' cooking, **combine** the butter and garlic in a small pot and simmer over low heat. Place the cooked fries in large bowl and **toss** well with the garlic butter, Parmesan, and parsley. **Add** a generous sprinkling of the kosher salt to taste, and **serve**.

Vegetable Fajitas

Makes 6

The perfect dish to introduce to your veggie-hating friends. But to get the real die-hard meat eaters to try it, you might need to say something like, "They're made with that new vegetable-shaped meat." They'll probably buy that.

1 tablespoon olive oil

1 green bell pepper, thinly sliced

1 red bell pepper, thinly sliced

½ large red onion, thinly sliced

1 medium-sized zucchini, thinly sliced

½ teaspoon ground cumin

½ teaspoon garlic powder

½ teaspoon cayenne pepper

6 flour tortillas, about 8 inches in diameter

½ cup sour cream

½ cup shredded Monterey Jack cheese

Preheat a large skillet over medium heat and add the olive oil. **Add** the green and red peppers and the onion and cook, stirring, until they begin to soften, about 5 minutes. **Add** the zucchini and cook, stirring, until everything begins to soften nicely, about 3 minutes more. **Add** the cumin, garlic, and cayenne and mix well. Turn down the heat and **warm** your tortillas in a nonstick pan or even briefly in the microwave. To **serve**, place a little sour cream, some vegetables, and a little cheese in each cooked tortilla, roll up, and **eat**.

Painless **Risotto**

Serves 6

Traditional risotto is a pain because you have to baby-sit it at the stove, very slowly stirring a ton of broth into it. My recipe is not traditional, but it's also not a pain. And it still comes out wonderful.

½ tablespoon olive oil

2 tablespoons small-diced yellow onion

1 clove garlic, chopped fine

1 cup Italian-style Arborio rice

⅓ cup dry vermouth

2 cups chicken broth

1 cup heavy whipping cream

⅓ cup freshly grated Parmesan cheese

4 tablespoons (½ stick) butter

Preheat the oven to 350°F. In a medium-sized ovenproof pot over medium heat, add the olive oil, then add the onion and garlic and cook, stirring, until softened but not brown, 3 to 4 minutes. Add the rice and mix until well coated, about a minute. Add the vermouth and cook, stirring, until the liquid has been absorbed, also about a minute. Stir in the chicken broth and cream and bring to a boil over medium heat. Cover with a lid and place in the oven for about 20 minutes, or until all the liquid has been absorbed and the rice looks creamy. Remove from the oven. Add the cheese and butter and stir in well.

Idiot Warning

Twice now I've forgotten that the handle of the ovenproof pot was hot and tried to remove it from the oven with my bare hands. Don't.

Just before serving, I like to drizzle it with a really good olive oil (see Really Good Olive Oil in Basic Stuff to Know on page 7), and give it a bit more cheese and some freshly ground black pepper.

Every so often we have an all veggie dinner and invite our carnivore friends... and we don't tell them it's veggie only. The funny thing is that they don't even notice, and when you tell them, they're all like "What, are you sure there wasn't some kind of meat or something?" And you're like "No dude, we went full-on no meat style—peace out."

My Favorite Way to Serve Artichokes

Makes 3 artichokes (serves 6 to 8 as an appetizer)

It's easy to forget that you can eat these prickly, goofy-looking things pretty much just the way they are. You always see them in pasta or a salad, but in my house, we like the leaves for dipping. Pulling, dipping, eating—artichokes are all about using your hands with food, and that's awesome.

3 artichokes

2 lemons, cut into 4 wedges each

4 tablespoons (½ stick) butter *stop your crying, you won't eat all the butter yourself*

1 cup mayonnaise

1 tablespoon curry powder

1 tablespoon prepared yellow mustard

2 tablespoons finely chopped fresh basil

1 fat clove garlic, chopped fine

Cut off the bottom stem of each artichoke, so that the artichoke can stand upright in the pot. Then cut about 1 inch off the top of each. Snip the sharp points off each leaf with scissors. **Stand** the artichokes, leaves pointing upward, in a large pan with water coming about halfway up them. **Squeeze** the lemons over the artichokes, and then throw the lemon wedges in the pan, but

save one wedge for making a dip. Bring to a **boil** over medium heat, then turn the heat down to a simmer, cover, and **cook** for about 45 minutes. They're ready when you can easily pull a leaf off the artichoke and pull the meat off the wide end of the leaves. **Remove** from the water, cool, and **serve** with all three dipping sauces. Yes, all three—variety is the key here.

Dipping Sauce 1: The butter, melted—so simple, so right.
Dipping Sauce 2: Combine half the mayo with the curry powder and mustard and mix well.
Dipping Sauce 3: Combine the remaining mayo with the basil, garlic, and juice from the remaining lemon wedge and mix well.

Now all you do is **pull** off a leaf (if they don't come off easily, they're not cooked enough), **dip** the wide part in one of the sauces, then use your teeth to sort of **scrape** the meat of the artichoke off the end of the leaf.

I think kids hate vegetables because their first experience with them is cold and all mashed up in a jar. Can you blame them?

Roasted Potatoes with Feta

Serves 6 to 8

Fragrant and crispy little potato pieces topped with feta and olive oil. Holy crap! Mrs. Cooking Guy—we'll call her Kelly—asks for these often. Of course I oblige only about one out of every four or five times. Hey, I can't have her thinking I'm her personal chef, can I?

2 pounds small red potatoes, quartered

1 large red onion, peeled and cut into a big dice like the potatoes

4 cloves garlic, crushed

2 tablespoons chopped fresh rosemary

2 tablespoons extra virgin olive oil, plus extra for serving

6 ounces feta cheese, crumbled

Preheat the oven to 450°F. Put the potatoes, onion, garlic, rosemary, and oil in a large bowl and **mix** well. **Dump** everything onto a baking sheet, spread out, and put in the oven. **Bake** until brown and crispy, about 45 minutes, but don't burn them. **Remove** from the oven, place on a serving tray or plates, and top with the feta and a good drizzle of olive oil.

Not-Boiled Double Cabbage

Serves 6

"Boiled cabbage": those two little words can strike culinary fear in the hearts of millions. "Here you go, honey, a nice bowl of wilted, mushy leaves." I don't get it, so I don't make it—or at least not like that. I'm all for cabbage. I love it in my Shrimp Tacos (page 128), but I like a crispy version that hasn't had the taste boiled out of it. And I use both purple and green cabbage, so it looks good, too. It's an interesting concept—food that tastes *and* looks good. Someone should clue in the boiled-cabbage people. It also makes a beautiful little bed to put things on, like big, fat grilled brats, or try the Maple Chops (page 156).

1 tablespoon peanut oil

2 cups thinly sliced green cabbage

2 cups thinly sliced purple cabbage

2 tablespoons brown sugar

1 teaspoon freshly ground black pepper

Preheat a large skillet or wok over high heat until very hot, then add the oil. When it begins to smoke **add** the cabbage. **Stir** it around so it cooks evenly—it will wilt a bit, but we want it still kinda crispy—about 5 minutes. When the cabbage is close to where you want it, **add** the brown sugar and pepper, **stir** very well for another minute, and **serve**.

Note: When slicing the cabbage, try to keep from using the thick-ish end near the core.

Wine as a present? No way. Forget taking a bottle of wine to someone's home as a gift—how about giving a bottle of really good extra virgin olive oil and a fresh baguette instead? You can get a great oil for somewhere around $20, and it says so much more than wine, mostly that you have an imagination...

Chili Lime Corn

Makes 8 ears *(I love saying that)*

This has a really nice bite for grilled corn. Making this outside in the middle of a snowstorm in February will make you think of summer. You'll freeze your butt off, but you'll still be thinking of summer.

8 ears of corn

1 cup (2 sticks) butter

2 tablespoons chili powder

Juice from 4 limes

1 to 2 tablespoons kosher salt

Preheat the grill to medium. **Pull** the husk and silk completely off the ears of corn. In a small pot over low heat, **melt** the butter. **Stir** in the chili powder and juice from 3 of the limes and **mix** well. **Grill** the corn right on the BBQ until soft, nicely browned, *and bitchin' looking*—this can take up to 30 minutes. Start **basting** with the seasoned butter about 10 minutes in, then baste often until the corn is soft enough to eat. When done, **remove** from the grill to a bowl or platter, **squeeze** the last lime on top, **sprinkle** with the salt to taste, and **serve**.

Great Grilled Veggies

Makes however much you want

There's just something awesome about veggies simply done on the BBQ. If it looks like a lot of work, it's not. You just cut up a bunch of whatever, then baste it while it's cooking—simple. Even the most die-hard vegetable hater will like these. And for the really stubborn cases, I suggest you start them with an appetizer of my Red Beer (page 149). It works wonders.

Basting ingredients

8 tablespoons (1 stick) butter

½ cup olive oil

2 tablespoons chopped fresh thyme, or 1 tablespoon dried thyme *you always use less dried, as it's just more concentrated*

2 tablespoons Dijon mustard

Juice of 1 lemon

1 bunch green onion (scallions), white and light green parts only, finely chopped

Vegetables

Green onions *just with the little fuzz at the bottom nipped off*

Japanese eggplant, cut lengthwise into ½-inch-thick slices

Red, yellow, or green bell peppers, cut into 3-inch strips

Asparagus, whole, but with the tough ends trimmed off

Fresh ears of corn, with husks and silks removed, cut crosswise into 4 pieces

Red onion, peeled and cut into thick round slices

Zucchini, with ends trimmed, cut in half crosswise, then quartered lengthwise

Preheat the grill well to medium-high. Put all of the basting ingredients in a small saucepan and heat over medium heat, stirring occasionally, until smooth and well combined. Add the vegetables to the grill and baste with the sauce.

Tip:

Put the heartiest veggies on the grill first because they'll take longer. For example, bell peppers always go on ahead of anything else.

At this point it's a free-for-all. Your goal is even cooking and basting—that's it. Softened veggies are good and so are grill marks—completely black and shrunken vegetables are not. Basically you want to baste and keep turning to make sure they don't burn. Remove the veggies to a platter when done and serve, remembering that "presentation is everything." Actually, my mother would argue that marrying a Jewish girl is everything, but this isn't her book, is it?

The Great
Potato Cake

Serves 6 to 8

Thin, crispy, well-seasoned little layers of potatoes—sounds like potato chips, doesn't it? Well,
it's not. It's like cake, in the sense that it comes
out of a pan when done and you cut and serve
it in wedges. I suggest a little caviar to finish
it, but don't go buying expensive caviar—it's
not necessary in this case. I buy the black
whitefish caviar from the supermarket, and
it works just fine.

2 large russet potatoes

4 tablespoons (½ stick) butter, melted

Kosher salt and freshly ground black pepper

For garnish

½ cup sour cream

2 tablespoons caviar

**2 green onions (scallions), green parts only,
chopped fine**

Preheat the oven to 450°F. **Wash**, peel, and slice the
potatoes into very thin rounds—about ⅟₁₆ of an inch—an
inexpensive slicer thing (aka mandoline) is perfect here.
A 7- or 8-inch cast-iron pan or ovenproof pot works really
well for this. **Butter** the bottom and sides really well.

Important

Unless you want all your hard work to wind up stuck in the pot, you'll take me seriously when I say to butter the bottom and sides "really" well.

Layer the potato slices in concentric circles on the bottom of the pan. Brush with the butter and sprinkle with salt and pepper. Repeat layering of potatoes with butter, salt, and pepper until you're out of potatoes—4 or 5 layers—then brush with butter and season with more salt and pepper one last time. Bake for 45 minutes with a small but heavy pot on top of the potatoes—this will help keep it cakelike. Then remove the top pot and turn up the oven to 500°F for 15 minutes more. Carefully invert onto a platter and, voilà—it looks like a cake, sort of. Cut into wedges and serve with a spoonful of the sour cream, a little caviar, and a sprinkle of chopped green onions.

Clean as You Go

There are a couple of different thoughts on cleaning in the kitchen. The first is what I practice—the "clean as you go" method. If you're waiting for a pot to boil or chicken to brown in the pan or whatever and find you have a minute or two, clean something. You'll be so much happier later that you did. The other way is what Mrs. Cooking Guy practices—I call it the "mess as you go and leave everything for Sam" method. It's definitely a method, so I can't fault her there...

The Best Asparagus

Serves 4

This is the only way to make asparagus, and you can serve them with pretty much everything. These are even good at room temp on a buffet table. Come to think of it, I love everything on a buffet table. Except for that awful gelatin "mold" thing my mom would make; it was just wrong. Not to mention the fact that it's named after something bad.

1 pound medium asparagus, with tough ends cut off

2 teaspoons olive oil

Kosher salt and freshly ground black pepper

Preheat the oven to 425°F. **Place** the asparagus on a baking sheet, **drizzle** with the olive oil, and **season** well with salt and pepper. **Roast** in the oven until just tender, which, depending on their size, will be between 10 and 15 minutes— you're going for "crisp-tender."

Note: *The other option is to cook the asparagus on your BBQ over medium heat until crisp-tender.*

Put on a nice platter and **serve**.

My Favorite Shiitakes

Serves 4

If shiitakes were a woman, they'd have the smoothest, most luxurious-feeling skin ever. *My wife just read that line and called me a moron.* I just mean that when you cook them, they get so . . . smooth and luxurious, I guess. These are tremendous at the side of a steak, or amazing with The Best Asparagus (at left).

1 tablespoon olive oil

1 pound fresh shiitake mushrooms, with stems removed, thinly sliced

1 teaspoon finely chopped garlic

2 tablespoons dry vermouth

1 tablespoon soy sauce

1 tablespoon butter

Preheat a wok or heavy skillet over medium-high heat and add the oil. Then add the mushrooms and garlic and cook, stirring occasionally, until softened, 7 to 10 minutes. Add the vermouth *off the heat—you don't want a flare-up*, stir until evaporated, then return to the heat. Add the soy sauce and butter, mix well, and serve.

Brussels Sprouts You'll Actually Eat

Serves 4

Brussels sprouts have gotten a bad rap for far too long—some of it totally deserved, I'll admit, but maybe we all just needed a different way of cooking them.

¾ pound Brussels sprouts

½ tablespoon olive oil

2 cloves garlic, crushed

½ teaspoon red pepper flakes

1 tablespoon balsamic vinegar

1 tablespoon brown sugar

Trim the sprouts to remove any ugly outer leaves. If the sprouts are large, like big walnuts, **cut** them in quarters lengthwise; if they're small, like a big grape, just cut them in half lengthwise. Bring a large pot of water to a **boil** over medium heat, place the sprouts in a steamer basket, place the basket in the pot, and **cover**. **Steam** until the sprouts are just beginning to get tender, about 10 minutes, then **drain**. **Preheat** a nonstick pan well over medium-high heat and **add** the oil. When it just begins to smoke, add the sprouts, garlic, and pepper flakes. **Stir** and keep moving until they begin to get a bit brown, maybe 2 minutes. **Add** the balsamic vinegar and brown sugar, stir for a minute, remove, and serve.

Cucumber Soup
(with Mint & Yogurt)

Serves 4

I really love this, and just because it's a cold soup doesn't mean it's only for summertime. Slice up a baguette, brush it with olive oil, and grill it—it's fantastic served with this soup.

2 English cucumbers, peeled and seeded
   (save a little for garnish)
½ cup mint leaves
1 clove garlic
¼ cup milk
1½ cups plain yogurt
1 tablespoon fresh lemon juice
Kosher salt and freshly ground black pepper
Extra virgin olive oil

Add the cucumber, mint, garlic, and milk to a blender. **Process** until smooth, then pour into a large bowl. **Stir** in the yogurt and lemon juice and season with salt and pepper. **Place** some finely chopped cucumber in the middle of each bowl for garnish. **Drizzle** lightly with really good extra virgin olive oil before serving.

I'm not one of those

Desserts

"Oh my god, if I don't get dessert I'm going to die" freaks. Did I say **freaks**? I meant people . . . wonderful, considerate, intelligent, and thoughtful people. But I do like a little something sweet after I eat sometimes. And I mean a little, so I like to make small portions because they look cool and because, when it comes to dessert, a little is better for you than a lot. A few bites—trust me—is really all you need.

Ice-Cream Grilled Pound Fruit (Fake) Hot Peaches Whole Pear Tart Pudding Mango Doughnutmisù and Blueberry Toffee Matzoh Ice-Cream Cup

Sandwich Deal
Cake with Fresh
Crème Brûlée
Easy Buñuelos
Chocolate Bread
Dessert Tacos
Grilled Peach
Pie Chocolate
Peanut Butter
Things

Ice-Cream Sandwich Deal

Serves 4

So it's not the most sophisticated name I've ever come up with, but just wait until you see it. Besides, it's made with those wacky ice-cream sandwiches. Honestly, it ends up looking like a bunch of snooty French guys worked on it for three days—but you made it in about thirty seconds.

4 tablespoons Hershey's chocolate syrup

4 plain vanilla ice-cream sandwiches

4 chocolate-mint cookies *Girl Scout Thin Mints are ideal*

1 tablespoon powdered sugar *also called confectioners' sugar*

Drizzle the chocolate syrup decoratively on each plate—back and forth, zigzag, whatever. **Slice** the ice-cream sandwiches in half, not lengthwise but . . . shortwise... *I don't really know how else to say that*. I just mean across the middle. Then slice each half diagonally to create 4 triangle-ish things. **Place** the cookies in a resealable plastic bag and zip shut. **Smash** into chunky crumbs with the bottom of something heavy. **Stand** 4 of the triangles up decoratively on the chocolate syrup in the middle of each plate. **Sprinkle** the cookies over the top, then give 'em a quick dusting of the powdered sugar, and eat—with your hands, of course.

Note: This is the one dessert we can always make in my house because we keep the ingredients around—so you can, too. It's like the perfect "Hey, why don't you come back to our place, I just remembered what we can have!" kinda thing.

Grilled Pound Cake
with Fresh Fruit

Serves 6

My mother taught me the joys of toasted and buttered pound cake. We'd stand in the kitchen toasting, buttering, and eating—and it's a wonder I don't weigh six thousand pounds. This is a version of that, but with no butter, and it has fruit to trick you into thinking it's healthy.

1 cup whipping cream

2 tablespoons Chambord (raspberry liqueur)

Six 1-inch-thick slices of store-bought pound cake

2 cups assorted fresh berries—blue, rasp, straw *you get the idea*

2 tablespoons Sugar in the Raw *that really chunky sort of crystallized brown sugar, which, as my editor would like to point out, is also known as "turbinado"—he so needs to get out more*

Put the whipping cream and Chambord in a bowl and **beat** with an electric mixer until thick. **Set** aside in the fridge. **Preheat** the grill to medium and grill the cake slices on both sides— *grill marks are good here*. Place the slices on serving plates and **top** with some of the Chamborded whipped cream and a big bunch of the mixed berries. Top it all with a light sprinkle of the Sugar in the Raw and **serve**.

Note: No grill available? Use your toaster or broiler to get the cake all cool—it's not how you get there, but how you end up.

(Fake) Crème Brûlée

Serves 4

Okay, so maybe this is not exactly the same as the real thing, but neither is the amount of work. This crème brûlée is made with those little pudding cups you send the kids to school with and is perfect to serve to those annoying neighbors who think they know everything about food—the "Oh, you simply *must* go to Tuscany, the *panna cotta* is divine" types. I just wanna smack them.

4 vanilla pudding cups

4 tablespoons sugar

8 fresh raspberries

Powdered sugar for dusting at the end

Fill 4 small ramekins almost to the top with the pudding, smooth the tops, and refrigerate for at least a couple of hours. Do this before the snots come over. Preheat the broiler (if you don't have one of those mini culinary blowtorches). Sprinkle a tablespoon of sugar evenly over each pudding. If using a culinary torch *a regular plumber's blowtorch will work, but be really careful!*, burn the top until the sugar melts and caramelizes to a golden, crusty brown.

If using the broiler, place the ramekins on a baking sheet and place them under the broiler; watch carefully through the oven window. Once the top is browned, return the ramekins to the refrigerator and chill until the topping hardens, at least 20 minutes. Then serve with a couple of raspberries on the side and a light dusting of powdered sugar. *Who's the foodie now?*

Heat Changes Things

So maybe this is like the most obvious concept in the history of man, but it's true. The best example I can give is of pound cake. In fact, check out the Grilled Pound Cake with Fresh Fruit recipe. The simple fact is that when you heat it, it completely changes. Same with deli meat—as in, heating it is wonderful. But not with tequila. Tequila plain is fine—tequila on the rocks is great.

Hot Peaches

Serves 4

Who wouldn't like this: warm brown-sugared peaches melting vanilla ice cream? And contrary to what you're thinking, this was not named after a stripper from the seventies—and you should be ashamed of yourself for even thinking that. By the way, her name was Galaxy.

1 tablespoon unsalted butter

2 large ripe peaches, sliced into thin wedges, or 2 cups frozen peaches, defrosted

2 tablespoons brown sugar

Juice of ½ lemon

Vanilla ice cream, the good stuff

Heat a nonstick pan over medium heat and melt the butter. When the butter starts to bubble, **add** the peaches and **cook** until thoroughly warmed and beginning to get some color, 5 to 10 minutes. **Add** the brown sugar and lemon juice and **stir** in well. **Remove** from the heat and **serve** over vanilla ice cream.

Easy
Buñuelos

Makes 12 pieces

Buñuelos are a crispy, totally delicious cinnamon-sugared fried Mexican dessert. But there are a few differences between the traditional buñuelos and mine:

Traditional buñuelos: homemade dough

My buñuelos: store-bought dough

Traditional buñuelos: deep-fried and difficult

My buñuelos: baked and simple

I could go on, but what would be the point?

1 frozen puff pastry sheet (from a package of 2)

1 cup sugar

1 tablespoon cinnamon

Remove the pastry sheet from the package and thaw at room temperature for about 30 minutes. Meanwhile, preheat the oven to 400°F. In a bowl combine the sugar and cinnamon and mix well. Unfold the pastry sheet and cut roughly into twelve 3 × 3–inch pieces. Place on an ungreased baking sheet and bake until puffy and golden brown, 10 to 15 minutes. Remove from the oven, toss in the cinnamon-sugar just to coat slightly, and serve.

Note: These are unbelievable with coffee—a good, strong espresso would be perfect. And notice that there's no x in espresso.

Whole Pear Tart

Not "whole pears," just a "whole big tart" full of 'em.

1 frozen puff pastry sheet (from a package of 2)

3 firm but ripe pears, peeled and sliced into ¼-inch slices *I slice down the sides—avoiding the core, of course—in order to get as many full pear-shaped slices as possible*

1 tablespoon cinnamon

1 tablespoon sugar

1 tablespoon unsalted butter

1 tablespoon honey

Remove the pastry sheet from the package and thaw at room temperature for about 30 minutes. Meanwhile, **preheat** the oven to 400°F. Place the pastry sheet on a lightly floured surface and **roll** out slightly. You're just trying to make it slightly bigger, by about an inch on all sides. **Poke** the pastry all over with a fork (this will keep it from getting too puffy), leaving a ½-inch border unpoked, and place on a lightly greased baking sheet. **Spread** out the pear slices evenly and as decoratively as you can on top of the pastry. **Combine** the cinnamon and sugar and **sprinkle** over the pear slices. **Bake** for about 15 minutes. **Melt** the butter with the honey in a small pot over low heat, or in a bowl in the microwave, and then **brush** over the tart. Continue baking until golden brown all over, about 10 minutes more. **Transfer** it to a serving platter and bring it to the table whole, cutting it there—it's gonna look awesome, so why waste the money shot alone in the kitchen?

Chocolate
Bread Pudding

Serves 8

Neither bread nor pudding, really—this is comfort dessert at its best. But don't say no to it because you don't like the idea of a pudding made with bread—like a certain someone in my family who will remain nameless. Difficult and picky, but nameless.

1 tablespoon butter

1 loaf cinnamon bread, sliced and cut into 1-inch cubes

½ cup pecan pieces

½ cup semisweet chocolate chips

3 large eggs, beaten

2 cups milk *I use 2 percent*

2 cups half-and-half

1 cup sugar

4 ounces whiskey or dark rum (optional)

Preheat the oven to 350°F. Lightly **butter** a 9 × 13–inch casserole dish. Put the bread cubes in the casserole dish and **toss** with the nuts and chocolate chips. **Combine** the eggs, milk, half-and-half, and sugar, **mix** well, and **pour** over the bread. Take your fingers and kind of **squish** the bread down a bit so everything gets moistened. **Bake** until set and no longer jiggly in the middle when you shake the pan, 30 to 40 minutes. Let **cool** slightly and **serve** in a bowl, not because it's pudding—because it's not. It's just more comforting in a bowl. If using the whiskey or rum, this would be the time to **drizzle** a little over the top of each serving.

Mango Dessert Tacos

Serves 4

Simple, messy, and gooey—just like dessert should be. No one gets a fork, no one, I say!

3 tablespoons granulated sugar

1 tablespoon cinnamon

4 flour tortillas, about 8 inches in diameter

2 tablespoons unsalted butter, softened

1 pint really good vanilla ice cream (see Note)

2 cups fresh ripe mango, peeled, with pit removed, and diced

¼ cup honey

Juice of ½ lemon

Powdered sugar

In a bowl, **combine** the granulated sugar and cinnamon and **mix** well. **Brush** both sides of the tortillas lightly with butter and **sprinkle** well with the cinny-sugar. **Heat** a nonstick skillet over medium heat and cook the tortillas on both sides until slightly crispy and brown. **Remove** to a serving plate. Put a **scoop** of ice cream on each tortilla and then **top** with some of the diced mango. **Drizzle** with the honey and a squeeze of the lemon juice, then a final **sprinkle** of the powdered sugar. Now just **fold** and **eat** as if it's the world's messiest, most delicious taco.

Note: I stress the "really good" part when it comes to choosing an ice cream because it really makes a difference. The difference between "really good" and "just okay" ice cream is like the difference between a "really good" chocolate cake and a pair of "old boxer shorts." Get it?

Doughnutmisù

Think tiramisù, but with powdered doughnuts.
Yes, it's that simple. And a pretty bitchin' name,
I might add.

1 cup mascarpone cheese, basically a triple
   cream cheese
¼ cup whipping cream
2 tablespoons powdered sugar, plus more
   for sprinkling
12 tablespoons Hershey's chocolate syrup
12 small powdered doughnuts, split in half the
   way you'd split a bagel
½ cup Kahlúa®
Unsweetened cocoa powder

Combine the mascarpone, whipping cream, and 2 tablespoons powdered sugar in a bowl and **blend** with an electric mixer until smooth. You'll need 12 small bowls (preferably glass); martini glasses work beautifully. **Put** 1 tablespoon of the chocolate syrup in the bottom of each bowl. **Dip** the cut side of each doughnut in the Kahlúa. On top of the chocolate in each small bowl, **place** 1 dipped doughnut half, then a heaping tablespoon of the mascarpone mixture, then another dipped doughnut half, then more mascarpone mixture, then **dust** with cocoa powder and a final light dusting of powdered sugar. If not serving right away, **refrigerate**, without the cocoa and powdered sugar but take them out about 20 minutes before you need them—there's nothing worse than an ice-cold Doughnutmisù. Cocoa and powder them before serving.

Grilled
Peach and
Blueberry Pie

Serves 8 to 10

This is grilled, as in "on the BBQ." The thing to do is to have it ready to go and just throw it on the grill when your main course comes off, and thirty-ish minutes later, it'll be ready.

2 ripe peaches, peeled, then sliced in about 16 wedges each

1 small basket fresh blueberries

3 tablespoons sugar

3 tablespoons flour

Grated zest from 1 lemon *just the yellow part of the peel*

One 9-inch ready-made pie crust (fresh, not frozen), uncooked

1 large egg, beaten

Preheat the grill to medium-high. In a bowl, **combine** the peaches, blueberries, 2 tablespoons of the sugar, 1 tablespoon of the flour, and the lemon zest and **mix** carefully so you don't mash up the fruit. Mashed fruit totally blows. **Fold** a piece of aluminum foil in half (large enough to accommodate the crust) and **dust** with the remaining flour. **Lay** the pie crust on top.

Place the fruit mixture in the center of the crust and fold the sides of the crust around it, making a sort of a series of pleats—it will not totally cover the fruit but will come a couple of inches toward the center, like a rustic tart. **Brush** the edges of the dough with the beaten egg and **sprinkle** with the remaining sugar. Carefully **lift** and place the foil with the pie onto the grill over indirect heat—that just means not directly atop the flames, if possible. Close the grill lid and **cook** until the dough is beautifully browned and the fruit has softened, about 30 minutes. Carefully **remove** to a serving platter. **Bring** to the table, graciously **accept** the applause, and humbly **deliver** your words of thanks.

Talk about confusing... desert and dessert. One is dry and sandy, and the other is—hey, actually, I've had a few desserts that were just like that!

Chocolate Toffee Matzoh

Makes a bunch (about enough for 20 people)

A classic Passover treat that's great any time—
and you don't even need to be Jewish to enjoy it.
If this had fallen from the heavens instead of
manna, I'm pretty certain the Jews would still be
in the desert right now waiting for more.

5 sheets of plain matzoh

½ pound (2 sticks) unsalted butter

1 cup light or dark brown sugar

¾ cup semisweet chocolate chips

¾ cup finely chopped pecans

Preheat the oven to 350°F. **Line** a couple of cookie sheets
with foil *it's gonna be a mess* and **top** that with
parchment paper if you have it—it gets really gooey and sticky.
Lay enough matzohs on the parchment paper to **cover** the
entire surface—you'll need to break some in half to fit the gaps.
Melt the butter and brown sugar in a saucepan over medium
heat, **stirring** constantly. Let the mixture come to a **boil**, turn
down the heat slightly, and continue cooking for 3 more minutes.
Remove from the heat and **pour** over the matzoh, covering
all. **Bake** for 15 minutes. **Remove** from the oven and quickly
sprinkle the chocolate chips over the top. Let the chips melt for

a couple of minutes, then **spread** the melted chocolate with the back of a spoon. You're looking to get chocolate just over the top of the matzoh—it doesn't need to cover it completely, but a little chocolate in each bite is a good thing. **Sprinkle** the nuts over the top of the chocolate and **press** down lightly so they stick. **Refrigerate** until set, then break into smaller pieces, and **look out**—as in "look out 'cuz it's so darn good you might eat it all yourself."

Don't eat everything in front of you. Just because food is there doesn't mean you have to eat it. Let me put it this way—if you make a recipe that says "Serves 5," and you find you've eaten the whole thing yourself, there's either an issue with the recipe...or you. I'd start by looking in the mirror...

Peanut Butter Ice-Cream Cup Things

Serves 6

I'll admit it: another bad name, but another great recipe. And with only four ingredients, it makes something very special. Oh, sure, you could go buy some ice-cream thing for dessert, but just wait until everyone sees how this looks and tastes—and then realizes you made it yourself.

2 cups really great vanilla ice cream, softened
½ cup peanut butter *I'd go with creamy*
½ cup whole salted peanuts, shelled
Hershey's chocolate syrup *in a squeeze bottle*

Cut and fit 6 pieces of wax paper large enough to cover the bottoms and sides, and to hang way over the edge, into six 7-ounce glasses or cups. **Spoon** ⅙ cup (about 2½ tablespoons) of the ice cream into the bottom of the glasses or cups and **press** down a little to flatten. **Melt** ½ the peanut butter in a small pan over low heat (or in the microwave), then **drizzle** a little over the ice cream in each cup. **Cover** each with the whole peanuts; you'll use about half of 'em. At this point, I stick it in the freezer for about 10 minutes. Then **add** the rest of the ice cream to each cup and flatten. Put in the freezer right away, for about an hour. When you're ready to serve, **melt** the remaining peanut butter and **drizzle** it decoratively on the bottom of 6 serving plates. **Turn** the ice-cream bundles out of the glasses and **remove** the wax paper. **Place** each inverted bundle neatly on a serving plate. **Drizzle** the Hershey's syrup creatively over the ice-cream bundle in a decorative, back-and-forth, "I'm a fancy chef" sort of way. **Chop** the remaining peanuts, **sprinkle** over the top, and **serve**.

Index